SIX THEATRE-IN-EDUCATION PROGRAMMES

Introduced and Edited by

CHRISTINE REDINGTON

DIRTY RASCALS
PEACEMAKER
UNDER EXPOSURE
THE SCHOOL ON THE GREEN
QUESTIONS ARISING IN 1985 FROM A MUTINY IN 1789
LIVES WORTH LIVING

A METHUEN PAPERBACK

First published in Great Britain in 1987 as a Methuen paperback original by Methuen London Ltd, 11 New Fetter Lane, London EC4P 4EE
Introduction © 1987 by Christine Redington
Dirty Rascals © 1987 by Leeds Playhouse Theatre in Education Company
Peacemaker © 1987 by David Holman
Under Exposure © 1987 by Lisa Evans
The School on the Green © 1987 by Greenwich Young Peoples Theatre
Questions Arising in 1985 from a Mutiny in 1789 © by Action PIE, Cardiff
Lives Worth Living © 1983 by Lawrence Evans and Jane Nash

British Library Cataloguing in Publication Data

Six theatre-in-education programmes.
　(A Methuen theatrefile)
　1. Children's plays, English　2. English, drama
　twentieth century
　I. Redington, Christine
　822'.914'08　　　PR1272

　ISBN 0-413-15790-3

The photograph on the front cover by Martin Mayer shows
Zak *from the play Dirty Rascals.*

Printed in Great Britain by
Richard Clay Ltd, Bungay, Suffolk

CONTENTS

INTRODUCTION

This collection of six Theatre in Education (TIE) programmes has brought together Infant, Junior and Secondary work that has been well tested by TIE companies and proved to be original, interesting and stimulating. It is *not* a 'top of the TIE pops' but sets out to show the range of subject matter and methods of work that have concerned TIE companies over the past six years.

In its choice of subject and form of presentation TIE differs from Children's Theatre. It selects contemporary or historical socio-political issues, not fantasy. The Junior programme in this volume, *Under Exposure,* investigates some of the problems of South Africa, whereas a Children's Theatre piece for the same age group may use a well-known children's story such as *Hansel and Gretel,* or invent a modern science-fiction fantasy. TIE companies work with small numbers of pupils, often just one class, and devise the programmes for a very specific age group. A Children's Theatre company may well perform to the whole Primary school, Infants and Juniors together, aiming to entertain and introduce theatre to young people.

TIE can be very entertaining but it sets out to do many other things and it uses theatre as a means, not an end in itself. A TIE programme is about the relationship between the pupils and the actor/teachers in the company, and how that relationship develops, how the company uses emotion and narrative to involve the pupils in the actions and lives of the characters. A programme can guide the pupils to use their intellects to analyse problems and to solve them if they can or, at least, to confront the fact that some problems are insoluble. TIE is about the opening up of a wider world for the pupil than just school and home, leading the pupils to question what they see and hear, and to draw their own conclusions. Within a TIE programme the actor/teachers may hand over the responsibility for decisions, actions or ideas to the pupils.

When Methuen published three volumes of TIE programmes in 1980 the Theatre in Education movement had been in existence for fifteen years. It had started in Coventry at the Belgrade Theatre, where for the first time a company of actor/teachers was set up to devise work especially for small groups of children in schools, playing to one class at a time, and asking teachers to follow through the work when the company left. From these beginnings the work spread throughout Great Britain and to Australia and New Zealand. It has never really taken hold in America which has its own Children's Theatre. Theatre in Education has its roots in the pioneer work of Caryl Jenner, Peter Slade and Brian Way and many more too numerous to begin to list here.

By 1980 the great increase in the number of companies was over and the future was looking less than rosy. Financial restraints and local Educational Authority cut-backs had led to the loss of TIE companies. This was mitigated somewhat by the introduction of the Government's Manpower Services Commission (MSC) funding, which could be used to pay the wages of a company wishing to perform in schools or the community. Obtaining MSC money for new companies today is much more difficult. However more Arts Council money has enabled new companies to be set up or existing ones to develop. The reason for this sudden increase of funding is due to the Arts Council's change of policy in 1984 announced in their document *The Glory of the Garden.* The main thrust of this new policy is to shift the weight of funding from London out to the regions and to begin to redress the balance between the funding of some art forms. The Arts Council focussed their financial support on a dozen or so areas within England where the population is most densely concentrated. The announcement of which companies should lose money and which areas should gain has caused much controversy. But for TIE the signs are hopeful as the Council proposes that, within the new development areas, increased funding should aid

Young People's Theatre. Although this new policy will help TIE to some extent it is counterbalanced by rate-capping cuts. Historically it was the Arts Council's decision in 1966 to fund Young People's Theatre for the first time that stimulated the expansion of Theatre in Education. It will be interesting to see whether the Council's second major change of policy will produce such results. The odds, alas, are against it.

Theatre in Education is vulnerable. Its funding comes partly from the Arts Council, or through them from the Regional Arts Associations, and from the local Education Authorities. Where the funding is adequate companies do not have to charge schools, as they see their work as part of education (if not part of the educational system). When they have to charge schools a fee for performances this puts pressure on the company to play to more than one class and this therefore changes the nature of the work. Funding for even the most established companies such as M6 can be threatened as local Authorities try to establish priorities for reduced funds. Such threats to grant support can cause companies to spend a great deal of energy just keeping themselves alive.

Due to its sources of funding TIE is vulnerable in another way: censorship. Theatre in Education deals with socio-political subjects, as the programmes in this volume illustrate. The commitment to such subject matter led the Gazebo TIE company in Wolverhampton to refuse Manpower Services Commission funding as that particular MSC area made several demands on the company about the subject matter they selected. Action PIE in Cardiff has recently been closed down. The reasons given were various. The company feel that it is a case of censorship. They have carried on working in schools after the closure on no pay. The script included in this volume was performed in schools before the closure of the company.

All this makes depressing reading, but TIE is far from depressing. At its best it is stimulating, thoughtful, responsible and theatrically and educationally innovative.

The scripts in this volume explore many subjects and techniques but all of them place an emphasis on the play. The bias is deliberate. Partly it reflects a trend in TIE that uses the play to stimulate drama workshops and discussion, rather than integrating this drama participatory work within the performance. *The School on the Green* by the Greenwich Young Peoples Theatre illustrates a variation on this pattern with its use of small sections of theatre or dialogue interspersed by discussion and pupil participation in the action. The emphasis on the TIE play within this volume is also a deliberate choice. It takes into account the difficulty a reader with little experience of Theatre in Education may experience when faced with a script which includes integral pupil participation. Where there is a great deal of audience participation within a programme the actual script can read as long passages of monologue by the actor/teachers, with the pupils' reactions and participation being briefly summarised. This does not offer the reader a true picture of what actually happened and anyone who has attempted to write up the range of activities and pupil responses that occurred within a good drama lesson will appreciate the problem.

The separate introductions by the company or writer will give the reader a sense of the context of the programme and its aims and achievements. The fact that the play appears dominant and the workshops that follow are only described in a few paragraphs is deceptive. It relates back to the point about summarising a good drama lesson. The workshops are *as important* as the play, for it is in these workshops that the pupils are able to explore, both intellectually and emotionally, the issues raised in the play. The workshops themselves use a number of techniques. One of the most popular is 'hot-seating', which entails the actor/teachers staying in character and being questioned as that character about their actions and opinions revealed during the play. The technique is popular because it can be so effective, with even sixth formers treating the actor/teacher as a real life character instead of a fictional one, and arguing

quite heatedly or being moved and worried by the character's problems.
The division into Infant, Junior and Secondary programmes is both for convenience
and to illustrate how techniques used for one age group can appear within a
programme for another age and still be as effective. *The School on the Green* uses
'depiction', a freezing of the dramatic action as if it were a photograph, which creates
an image. This image can then be analysed. It can also be unfrozen and the action run
forwards or backwards to enable the pupils to examine how that particular event
occurred or to view the result of the action. It is used in Greenwich Young Peoples
Theatre programme to analyse what is happening but also to lead into discussion on
the real reasons why Tom and Annie Higdon, the teachers at the Burston school, were
sacked. In *Questions Arising in 1985 from a Mutiny in 1789* the technique is used to
ask pupils questions but not to lead them into immediate discussions. The questions
are pertinent to 1985 and they leave the pupils to consider them after the play not
during it and to relate the historical events that they have witnessed to the events of
1985.

Depictions create theatrical images. Images can be more powerful and more
effective than words, and Theatre in Education companies make careful use of stage
properties or stage settings that can tell the pupils more about the subject and make
them react on many different levels. David Holman's play *Peacemaker,* written for
Infants, uses a wall as its central image. The wall is the barrier between peoples, a
physical as well as a mental barrier, but it can be taken down, contact and
understanding between different peoples, different Nations, can be made, prejudices
can be overcome.

Peacemaker tells a story; so does *Under Exposure.* The two programmes by GYPT
and Action Pie use history's own narrative.

Many TIE programmes have a strong story line, which keeps the pupils' attention
and adds to their involvement. However such programmes as *Dirty Rascals* and *Lives
Worth Living* are moments in peoples' lives. There is no real narrative, just characters,
conflicts, indecisions and a whole range of emotions. In *Dirty Rascals* the seven-year-
old audience watches seven-year-olds play and talk. It may seem odd to the reader that
grown actor/teachers are able to realistically portray such young children, but it can
be done. It not only requires very strong acting skills but also sincerity of intent and
presentation. This kind of acting is a long way from the children portrayed in some
forms of Childrens' Theatre, all red dots on cheeks, bows in hair, who caper and
bounce and speak in very loud squeaky voices. The children in *Dirty Rascals* have to
be real for the seven-year-olds watching to identify with them and their various
problems and emotions. Only then can the children fully explore their own ideas for,
and with, the characters during the workshop.

The research for *Lives Worth Living* led the two actor/teachers to realize the
amount of prejudice and ignorance that exists about mental handicap. To show this
and to demonstrate the problems that are involved in caring for the handicapped one
actor portrayed, as realistically as possible, a mentally handicapped young man. He did
this within the 'hot-seating' session too, thus giving the pupils the opportunity to
react to Mark as a real human being, not just an actor playing a character. There is no
action in the play. Mark and his sister Julie are on a beach. They talk, rest, react to
others. By being so simple in story the programme is more effective in its impact. The
issue of Mark's handicap and how he and those around him react to it dominates the
play.

The fact that Theatre in Education is prepared to tackle contemporary political
issues is illustrated by Lisa Evans' *Under Exposure,* which examines the lives of women
in the squatter camps in South Africa. This particular programme was written for

Theatre Centre's Women's Company. Theatre Centre consists of several companies; at their busiest time the number of actor/teachers employed can rise to eighteen. In 1983 the Women's Company was formed as a result of pressure from women within Theatre Centre who wanted to take an initiative in anti-sexist education by developing imagery and language of theatre from a female perspective. (It was also formed to create job opportunities for women in a male-dominated profession.) *Under Exposure* is thus both about the problems of South Africa, a very contemporary issue, and about the attitudes of women, both white and black. Theatre Centre also took an initiative in integrated casting, that is, casting which ignores skin colour. The company had become acutely aware of the contradiction of an all-white company playing to audiences of many different ethnic groups.

Although the programmes in this volume appear in isolation they must be seen in the context of the schools and the close relationship between the Theatre in Education team and teachers. Most TIE programmes have a set of Teachers' Notes that accompany them and offer the teacher a range of follow-up work, research material and discussion points. Many of the programmes were the result of consultations with teachers and the teacher is seen as essential in carrying on the ideas in the programme over a period of time. A few TIE teams have decided to work only with a limited number of schools so that they can build up real liaison with individual teachers and can share the creation and follow-up process with them. GYPT follow this policy, so does Cockpit. The Belgrade Company has set up a special project, initiated by its Schools Liaison Officer, whereby she actually teaches in three local schools.

TIE is not yet a widespread phenomenon. There are many companies who offer some form of childrens' entertainment and tour the country. TIE tends to work where it is based and establishes links with local schools. In spite of its funding problems TIE soldiers on and shows no signs of dying (a fate predicted for it by some pessimists). Neither does it show many signs of multiplying. It remains, however, the centre of very creative work, innovative techniques and a voice of conscience in a theatrical profession that often appears not to notice the events in the world around it.

Christine Redington, 1987

Select Bibliography

Theatre in Education

Arts Council of Great Britain, *The Provision of Theatre for Young People.* Chairman: Hugh Willatt, Arts Council, 1966.

Arts Council of Great Britain, *The Glory of the Garden,* Arts Council, 1984.

S. Craig. (ed.) *Dreams and Deconstructions,* Alternative Theatre in Britain (contains a chapter on Theatre in Education), Amber Lane Press, 1980.

T. Jackson, (ed.) *Learning Through Theatre,* Essays and Casebooks on Theatre in Education, Manchester University Press, 1980.

J. O'Toole, *Theatre in Education,* London, Hodder & Stoughton, 1976 (now out of print).

C. Redington, *Can Theatre Teach?,* An historical and evaluative analysis of Theatre in Education, Oxford, Pergamon Press, 1983.

B. Way, *Audience Participation,* Theatre for Young People, Boston, Walter H. Baker Co., 1981.

Theatre in Education programmes

Belgrade TIE, *Rare Earth,* London, Methuen, 1976 (for 9–11 yr. olds).

Belgrade TIE, *Killed,* Amber Lane Press, 1982 (for top secondary pupils).

Leeds TIE, *Raj,* Amber Lane Press, 1984 (for 10–12 yr. olds).

P. Schweitzer, *Theatre in Education,* 3 vols: *Five Infant Programmes, Four Junior Programmes, Four Secondary Programmes,* London, Methuen, 1980.

Articles relating to the scripts in this volume

M. Kenney, *Seeing the Water,* An analysis of the Leeds Playhouse programme 'Dirty Rascals' in *2D,* vol. 4, no. 1, Autumn 1984.

Theatre in Education journals

SCYPT Journal published by the Standing Conference of Young Peoples Theatre.

Theatre in Education programmes on Video

N. Duffield, *Brand of Freedom* presented by Pit Prop TIE Company, programme devised for 9–11 year olds, Manchester University Television Productions, 1984.

DIRTY RASCALS

Devised by Leeds TIE Company

A full day programme
for two classes of seven year olds

The Play: *Dirty Rascals* takes its title from a British children's game. The single rule of the game is that only one person can be top, and then not for long. A child claims status — 'I'm the king of the castle. You're the dirty rascals' — and is then pushed off.

The game is the central image of our play. The children in it, like all children in Britain, are 'dirty rascals', afforded little status and power. Throughout the play the characters constantly claim status: 'Have you got a video?'; 'What team do you support?'; 'I bet you don't know what that's called.' All claim status at another's expense. The aim of the day was to allow the children to explore status and power at a personal level, and the ways in which these are reflected in, and influenced by, the wider world.

The play was arrived at from a long period of improvisation. Research involved talking to, observing and delving into our own experiences of being seven year olds. Gradually three characters emerged and a high level of realism in their portrayal became important to the company.

For these characters certain issues surface, particularly in relation to gender, race and class. However the play is not intending to teach *about* these issues. They are present in the play because of the particular characters of Zak, Bimla and Stephen. It should not be assumed that they are always of prime importance either to the characters or to the children watching.

The Set was as realistic a representation of a derelict house as we could make it. The class sat around peering in over two of the broken walls. It was scaled up slightly in order to make the actors look more like seven year olds. It was littered with bits of junk culled from local derelict houses. All of it was real. All of it was used in the characters' games.

The Games — like the house — bring the adult world into the play. Families, schools, war are situations in which power is an issue, through which values and attitudes are transmitted, and which children themselves use to make sense of the world.

The Toys — the doll, the gun, the book, and the ammonite — although associated with particular characters, are the concrete objects over which negotiations over status take place.

Through these elements the play is intended to function at two levels, the real and the symbolic. But only so far as these levels actually coexist in life. In a sense, the play is about the relationship between the two.

Mike Kenny,
for Leeds TIE company, 1987

Dirty Rascals was first performed at Lincoln Green First School on 1 November 1983, with the following cast:

BIMLA   Annalyn Bhanji
STEPHEN   Mike Kenny
ZAK   Wyllie Longmore

Devising Company: Annalyn Bhanji, Biddy Coghill, Harry Duffin, Mike Kenny,
        Wyllie Longmore, Gail McIntyre, Christine Murdoch, Paul Swift

Written by Paul Swift
Directed by Gail McIntyre
Designed by Harry Duffin

Teachers' materials compiled by Biddy Coghill, Christine Murdoch, Paul Swift

Scene One: STEPHEN

STEPHEN *enters from the estate, looks over the wall, enters the space through the door frame. He picks up a couple of things; chooses a reasonably low object, tests it, then stands on it. He looks round.*

STEPHEN: I'm the king of the castle, get down you dirty rascals.

He looks round, gets down and sits. Takes out the ammonite, runs his fingers over it, puts it to his ear, looks around him again. Mumbles under his breath: 'this could be my castle, and these are the battlements', etc. He builds a castle from objects lying around, shouts: 'I'm the king of the castle' again, makes his 'dinner' and sits down to eat it.

Scene Two: STEPHEN and BIMLA

Enter BIMLA *from the old houses with plastic doll, book and bag of sweets. She watches* STEPHEN, *who stops, looks at her, then somewhat self-consciously continues.* BIMLA *steps over the wall.*

BIMLA: You shouldn't play in here.

STEPHEN: Why not?

BIMLA: 'Cos it's dangerous. Haven't you heard them, scratching?

STEPHEN: What?

BIMLA: The rats. Dirty great big ones, and if they bite you, you get a horrible disease and you die. So you'd better not play here. (*She re-arranges the objects.*)

STEPHEN: You're playing in there.

BIMLA: I like rats.

STEPHEN: I come from Dewsbury. We've just moved.

BIMLA: Into Nicola Page's house?

STEPHEN: That one over there.

BIMLA: Nicola Page's house. She's gone to Morley. She was my best friend and this was our secret den. You've got a sister called Maureen, haven't you?

STEPHEN: Yeah.

BIMLA: I talked to her. She looks after you, dunt she? You and your little brother?

STEPHEN (*nods*): She's eleven.

BIMLA: Do you like her?

STEPHEN: She's alright.

BIMLA: She's got a doll called Veronica. My doll's called Veronica. What's your name?

STEPHEN: Stephen. What's yours?

BIMLA: You live in a house, don't you Stephen?

STEPHEN: Yeah.

BIMLA: I don't.

STEPHEN: Do you live in a tent?

BIMLA: Course I don't, dafthead. I live in a shop, in the old houses. It's my dad's shop and it's full of sweets. Have you got a video?

STEPHEN: No.

BIMLA: We have.

STEPHEN: My mam's got a catalogue, and she can get you anything. She sends away.

BIMLA: Don't need to. My dad's shop sells everything.

STEPHEN: I bet it doesn't.

BIMLA: Does.

STEPHEN: Bet it doesn't sell computers.

BIMLA: Bet you daren't swing on there.

STEPHEN: Bet you daren't. (BIMLA *does.*)

BIMLA (*swinging*): See? (*Drops.*) You do it.

STEPHEN: Don't want to.

BIMLA: 'Cos you're scared.

STEPHEN: I'm not allowed to do dangerous things.

BIMLA: Why?

STEPHEN: 'Cos I broke my leg in three places, if you must know. At school in PE.

BIMLA: Did you cry? I bet you did.

STEPHEN: You'd have cried.

BIMLA: I wouldn't. I'd have screamed. Are you dead tough?

STEPHEN: No.

BIMLA: I am. (*Sees the ammonite.*) What's that?

STEPHEN: None of your business.

BIMLA: Show us.

STEPHEN: No.

BIMLA: Go on.

STEPHEN: No.

BIMLA: Don't then.

STEPHEN: It's an ammonite.

BIMLA: What's one of them?

STEPHEN: It's ancient. It's a creature that died millions and millions of years ago, and it fell to the bottom of the sea and got covered in sand and turned to stone.

BIMLA: You're kidding me.

STEPHEN: I'm not. Teacher told me. We did a project on it.

BIMLA: Can I hold it? I'll lend you my special book. (*Gives it to him.*) My grandad gave it to me. It's from India. Can I hold it then? (STEPHEN *gives the ammonite to her.*) Hey, you know what this is?

STEPHEN: It's an ammonite.

BIMLA: No, it's a magic stone. Are you playing?

STEPHEN: Alright. Castles.

BIMLA: House. I'm the mum and you're the dad, and this is Veronica, she's our baby, and you're reading her a story. And we live in this big posh house and we're dead rich.

STEPHEN: Do we have a video?

BIMLA: We have three.

STEPHEN: And computers in every room, and even one in the toilet.

BIMLA: Yeah. Go on then.

STEPHEN: What?

BIMLA: Read Veronica a story.

STEPHEN: I can't.

BIMLA: Why not?

STEPHEN: It's the morning and I've got to go to work. I'm a gasman.

BIMLA: You can't be a gasman.

STEPHEN: I can if I want.

BIMLA: Gasmen aren't rich, are they? And they smell.

STEPHEN: No they don't.

BIMLA: They smell of gas.

STEPHEN: They don't.

BIMLA: How do you know?

STEPHEN: My dad's a gasman.

BIMLA: Is he?

STEPHEN: Yeah.

BIMLA: Alright. You used to be a gasman, but now you own lots of shops. Yeah, you own Lewis's.

STEPHEN: Yeah.

BIMLA: So you don't need to go to work.

STEPHEN: What do I do then?

BIMLA: You stay at home and look after Veronica.

STEPHEN: What do you do?

BIMLA: I'm a doctor. I've got to work because I'm needed. It's night time now, and I come home.

STEPHEN: What's your name?

BIMLA: Bimla.

STEPHEN: Hello, Bimla.

BIMLA: Hello, Stephen love. (STEPHEN *screws up his face.*) What are you doing that for?

STEPHEN: Aren't you going to kiss me? My dad always kisses my mam when he comes home from work.

BIMLA: I bet she doesn't screw her face up though.

STEPHEN: Sorry. (BIMLA *kisses STEPHEN*.)

BIMLA: Hello Veronica. (*Kisses doll*.) Has she been good?

STEPHEN: I've not had a minute's peace with her. She cried all morning.

BIMLA: Do you think she's poorly?

STEPHEN: Yeah.

BIMLA: I'll give her some medicine. (*Takes out sweets, gives one to Veronica and eats it herself*.) There. She's better now. (*Pause. STEPHEN looks at sweets*.) Are you poorly?

STEPHEN: Yeah.

BIMLA: Here. (*Gives him a sweet*.) Are you cured?

STEPHEN: Yeah.

BIMLA: I'd better have one in case I catch it. Is my tea ready?

STEPHEN: Yeah. You hold Veronica and I'll get it.

BIMLA: Pooh, she's got a stinky nappy.

STEPHEN: You'll have to change it.

BIMLA: I can't do it. I've been curing people all day, I'm tired out.

STEPHEN: Well, I've been cleaning and washing and ironing and shopping . . .

BIMLA: No, you haven't. We're rich. We have servants to do that. You've just been playing with Veronica all day. (STEPHEN *takes the doll*.) Talk to her then.

STEPHEN: Come on, Veronica, we'll soon have you all clean. There's a good baby.

BIMLA: You've got it on your hands.

STEPHEN: Eer! It's on you now. (*Touches* BIMLA.)

BIMLA: Ah, she's crying.

STEPHEN: Don't cry, there's a good baby. You're all clean now.

BIMLA: Sing to her.

STEPHEN (*rocking the doll in his arms*): 'Bye baby bunting, Daddy's gone a-hunting, Gone to fetch a rabbit skin To wrap the baby bunting in.' She's asleep.

BIMLA: Where's my tea?

STEPHEN: I can't do everything at once, can I? I'll put her in her cot. (*Puts the doll down*.)

BIMLA: And don't forget to wash your hands.

STEPHEN (*gives* BIMLA *old tin can*): Here you are.

BIMLA: What is it?

STEPHEN: Dog food. (STEPHEN *giggles*. BIMLA *stares at him*.) Don't you eat dog food then?

BIMLA: No. Do you?

STEPHEN: No. (*Pause*.) I tasted some once.

BIMLA: What?

STEPHEN: Dog food.

BIMLA: What was it like?

STEPHEN: Slimey.

BIMLA: Eer! (BIMLA *smiles*.)

STEPHEN: It's not really dog food, I was kidding you. It's fish and chips really. (STEPHEN *eats*, BIMLA *joins in*.) Do you like it?

BIMLA: Yeah, it's great.

STEPHEN: I know, you go to the pub and you come home dead drunk.

BIMLA: Alright.

STEPHEN: What time do you call this then? And you're drunk again aren't you?

BIMLA: Yeah.

STEPHEN: How many pints have you had?

BIMLA: Hundreds.

STEPHEN: Well, I'm sick of it. Every night you've been down that pub, while I'm stuck in the house looking after the kids. It's not fair, is it?

BIMLA: No.

STEPHEN: No, you say, 'Well I go out to work, I need my relaxation.'

BIMLA: I go out to work, I need my relaxation.

STEPHEN: When do I get my relaxation?

BIMLA: I don't know.

STEPHEN: I *don't*! Your job finishes at half past five. Well my job never finishes. They're your kids an all, you know. Say, 'I'm going to bed'.

BIMLA: I'm going to bed.

STEPHEN: That's right, go off and leave me to it. Aw, look, the baby's crying now,

BIMLA: Is she poorly again?

STEPHEN: No, she's fed up.

BIMLA: Why?

STEPHEN: She's been bullied.

BIMLA: She can't have been bullied. She's only a baby.

STEPHEN: This isn't Veronica, it's Geoffrey. He's seven and a half and he's been bullied, so what you gonna do about it?

BIMLA: You should keep him in.

STEPHEN: That's not fair.

BIMLA: I know.

STEPHEN: And anyway he gets bullied at school, so what you gonna do?

BIMLA: You're the dad, you think of something.

STEPHEN: Do you get bullied?

BIMLA: Do you?

STEPHEN: Yeah.

BIMLA: So do I. Who bullies you?

STEPHEN: Some lads, they're dead rough. They say I'm teacher's pet, 'cos I like doing projects and I don't muck about, but I'm not. I told the teacher about them bullying me and he said it was my fault, and I should stop acting like a girl and stick up for myself. I can't help it if I don't mess about. And I like doing projects.

BIMLA: They only mess about because they can't do it. They're just thickos. That's why they bully you, because they're no good at anything else. I hate thickos.

STEPHEN: So do I. Why do you get bullied?

BIMLA: Jason Phillips hit me over the head with his tractor because he said I coughed posh. And them skinheads off your estate, they're always up here getting on to us.

STEPHEN: Why?

BIMLA: Why d'you think?

STEPHEN: Because you live in old houses?

BIMLA: No, because we're not white. (*Pause.*) Don't anybody stick up for you?

STEPHEN: Our Maureen sometimes. But she's gone to the middle school now.

BIMLA: I'll stick up for you.

STEPHEN: Will you? Really?

BIMLA: Yeah.

STEPHEN: I'll stick up for you an all.

BIMLA: Will you?

STEPHEN: Yeah.

BIMLA: We have to swear it, on the magic stone.

STEPHEN: Alright. (*They hold the ammonite together.*)

BIMLA: I swear.

STEPHEN: I swear.

BIMLA: I've got a secret place. Shall I show you?

STEPHEN: Yeah.

BIMLA: This hole here. We could put the magic stone in it.

STEPHEN: Can I do it?

BIMLA: No, I'd better. You get back.

STEPHEN: Why? (BIMLA *puts the stone in the hole.*)

BIMLA: 'Cos it's a rat hole. (STEPHEN *retreats.*)

STEPHEN: Get it out.

BIMLA: Why?

STEPHEN: 'Cos I've got to go home now. To see if my tea's ready.

BIMLA: It'll be safe in there till after.

STEPHEN: I might not be playing after. My dad might not let me.

BIMLA: Why not? (*Pause.*)

STEPHEN: He dunt like me playing with kids like you.

BIMLA: What d'you mean?

STEPHEN: Foreigners.

BIMLA: I'm not a foreigner.

STEPHEN: You are though.

BIMLA: I was born in Leeds, at St James's Hospital. Where were you born?

STEPHEN: Dewsbury.

BIMLA: And where are we now?

STEPHEN: Leeds.

BIMLA: So you're the foreigner, dafthead. You're the one who comes from Dewsbury and eats dog food! (*Pause.*) I'm sorry. I'll get it for you if you like.

STEPHEN: It'll do after.

BIMLA: What about your dad?

STEPHEN: If he asks me I'll tell him I was playing with Veronica.

BIMLA: See you after.

STEPHEN: Yeah. (*He picks up the book.*) See you, Bimla.

STEPHEN *exits.*

Scene Three: BIMLA

BIMLA: You sit there Veronica. (BIMLA *sits the doll and goes and gets the ammonite. To the doll.*) We have one wish each, alright? (*Places the stone with the doll. As Veronica.*) 'I wish I was real.' You daft doll, you're not supposed to tell anybody. It'll never come true now. My turn. (*Takes ammonite.*) I wish . . . (*Closes her eyes tight. Opens them, smiles. As Veronica.*) 'What did you wish, Bimla?' Not telling, it's a secret. I've got to put it back now.

She leaves the doll and is on her knees about to put the ammonite in the hole when she looks round to check if the coast is clear.

Scene Four: BIMLA and ZAK

ZAK *enters with gun from the direction of the new estate.* BIMLA *watches him from behind some rubble.* ZAK *is tearful and preoccupied with his gun. Just outside the house he stops, looks back towards the estate, pulls the trigger furiously.*

ZAK: It's broke now! You broke my gun, you rotten creep! I'll get you for this! When I'm bigger you'd better watch out, 'cos I'll smack you good and proper then! Nobody crosses Zak Taylor and gets away with it!

BIMLA: Who you talking to? (ZAK *secretively wipes the tears from his face.*) There's nobody there.

ZAK: So?

BIMLA: You must be crackers.

ZAK: Not as crackers as you, Bimla Seth.

BIMLA: You've been crying.

ZAK: I haven't.

BIMLA: You have.

ZAK: I haven't. (*Almost starting again. He turns away.*)

BIMLA: You have, you're doing it now.

ZAK: It's not proper crying. It's 'cos I'm mad. Rotten creep broke me gun. I only got it on Saturday and it don't spark now.

BIMLA: Who bashed you?

ZAK: Nobody.

BIMLA: Looks like it.

ZAK: Well you haven't seen the other kid. You don't know how they broke me gun, do you? They broke it with their head.

BIMLA: You'll get into trouble.

ZAK: I don't care. Rotten estate kids. They're always picking on us. They ask for it.

BIMLA: Why do you go there, then?

ZAK: Why shouldn't I? It's a free country, isn't it?

BIMLA: 'Cos you get into trouble. You must like getting into trouble. You're always doing it.

ZAK: What about you?

BIMLA: I'm not in trouble.

ZAK: I know something you don't know.

BIMLA: What?

ZAK: Not telling you, but when you get home you'll be for it.

BIMLA: Don't believe you.

ZAK: Don't then.

BIMLA: Don't care anyway. (*Pause. ZAK swings on the door frame.*) Anybody can do that.

ZAK: You can't.

BIMLA: Get down and I'll show you.

ZAK: Don't want to. I'm the cock of our street. I'm the cock of our school. There's nobody I can't beat up.

BIMLA: There's loads. Half the boys in class 4, all them skinheads.

ZAK: You can't count older kids.

BIMLA: Me.

ZAK: I can beat you up easy, if I wanted.

BIMLA: Come on then.

ZAK: Don't want to.

BIMLA: Because you can't. (ZAK *drops down, sizes up for a second, then backs down.*)

ZAK: You're a girl.

BIMLA: So?

ZAK: Girls don't count. (*Shoots* BIMLA *with gun.* BIMLA *doesn't react.*) You're dead.

BIMLA: No I'm not.

ZAK: I just shot you.

BIMLA: But I've got my magic stone. It melts bullets, so they can't hurt me.

ZAK: What is it?

BIMLA: Are you deaf? It's a magic stone.

ZAK: Let's have a look at it then.

BIMLA: Alright, if you can get it. (*Throws it in the hole.*) Go on, I dare you.

ZAK: It's easy.

BIMLA: Go on then. 'Cos they can't hurt you much, can they?

ZAK: What?

BIMLA: Rats. That's a rat hole. (ZAK *withdraws his hand quickly.*) Don't you like rats?

ZAK (*staring at the hole*): I'll get it.

BIMLA: I'll dare you something else then. I bet you daren't kiss me.

ZAK: I dare. (*Kisses her quickly.*) See.

BIMLA: In the school yard at playtime.

ZAK: I'll show you.

BIMLA: On Monday.

ZAK: On Monday. That's if you're still alive on Monday. (BIMLA *yawns extravagantly*.) Ravi's been looking for you all the afternoon. You're supposed to be looking after your little brother while your mum's at the market.

BIMLA: Was my little brother with him?

ZAK: No, he left him at the shop with your dad.

BIMLA: Aw heck. I bet he did it on purpose. He loves getting me into trouble our Ravi. And 'cos he's the eldest my mum and dad always believe him. He's a right creep.

ZAK: Like my sister. She's always telling tales. She says I'm a little pest and I'll end up in prison. I get into trouble even when I don't do anything and she gets away with murder.

BIMLA: I don't think our Ravi likes me.

ZAK: Marcia hates me. (*Pause*.) Do you want to play something.

BIMLA: Yeah, alright, so long as it's not guns and shooting.

ZAK: Why?

BIMLA: 'Cos it's boring. 'Bang you're dead' 'I got you' 'No you didn't' 'Yes I did'.

ZAK: Not if we're both on the same side. It's fun then.

BIMLA: Pretending to kill people?

ZAK: Yeah. You can have the gun.

BIMLA: I don't want to. It's stupid.

ZAK: Well I'm not playing babies.

BIMLA: Why not?

ZAK: 'Cos it's sissy.

BIMLA: It's not sissy, it's real. When you grow up you'll have babies won't you, but you won't go round shooting people.

ZAK: If there was a war you would.

BIMLA: No you wouldn't, you'd just press buttons, everybody knows that. (*Pause*.) Would you like to shoot people really?

ZAK: No. I wouldn't like to have babies neither.

BIMLA: School.

ZAK: Yeah, alright.

BIMLA: And I'll be Miss Coghill. This is our classroom and that's your seat there. This is the blackboard. (*As teacher*.) 'What are you doing Zak Taylor? Why aren't you sitting at your table?'

ZAK: I've got ants in my pants, Miss.

BIMLA: 'Sit down this minute. This is a classroom not a railway station.' (ZAK *makes train noises*.) 'Where were you Zak Taylor when God was giving brains out?'

ZAK: Don't know, Miss.

BIMLA: 'Playing around in the toilet I shouldn't wonder.'

ZAK: Yes, Miss. I was learning to wee over the wall, Miss.

BIMLA: You wouldn't dare say that to Miss Coghill.

ZAK: I would.

BIMLA: You wouldn't.

ZAK: I would.

BIMLA: Alright. 'Come out here Zak Taylor.'

ZAK: You just told me to sit down.

BIMLA: 'Come out here and hold out your hand.' (*Picks up a large piece of wood*.) 'You're going to get the ruler.'

ZAK: You're not hitting me with that.

BIMLA: Only pretend. (*Pretends to hit*.)

ZAK: Didn't hurt.

BIMLA: 'Pardon?'

ZAK: I just coughed, Miss.

BIMLA: 'Sit down. Now will the boys

please stop being silly, and get on with their work. Look at the girls. They're not being silly. They're getting on very nicely.'

ZAK: Bimla and Alison are talking, Miss.

BIMLA: 'Bimla, stop talking to Alison, or you'll go and sit on the bottom table with Zak Taylor. David is trying to work, aren't you David?'

ZAK (*using the doll*): 'Yes, Miss.' This is David Dunk.

BIMLA: 'Good boy David.'

ZAK: 'Please Miss Coghill, Bimla keeps hitting me, Miss.'

BIMLA: 'Letting the girls down again, Bimla. Come out here. Now that wasn't very lady-like, was it?' No, Miss. 'I've told you all before, I won't have hitting in my class. Hold out your hand.' (*Mimes hitting* BIMLA.) 'And the next person to misbehave will go and see Mr Turvey. Now, this morning 3C we're going to learn about babies.'

ZAK: We don't do that.

BIMLA: 'This morning we do. And Zak Taylor will show us how to hold one.' (*Offering doll.*)

ZAK: I won't.

BIMLA: You've got to.

ZAK: I won't.

BIMLA: Miss Coghill says. (ZAK *takes the doll and holds it by the leg upside down.*) 'You don't hold a baby like that.'

ZAK: I do, Miss. (*Makes the doll hit him.*) Ooh, it's hit me in the face, Miss. (*Struggles with it.*)

BIMLA: Stop it!

ZAK: It's not me, it's the baby, Miss. It's beating me up. (ZAK *staggers and falls pretending the doll is strangling him;* BIMLA *laughs at first, then wants him to stop.*)

BIMLA: Stop it! (ZAK *stops. The doll's arm has come off. Pause.*)

ZAK (*mumbling*): Sorry. (*Offers doll and arm to* BIMLA.)

BIMLA: You've broken her now.

ZAK (*mumbling*): Didn't mean to.

BIMLA: Mend it! (*Pause.*) I said, mend it.

ZAK: What if I don't?

BIMLA: You'd better!

ZAK: Why? What'll you do? Beat me up?

BIMLA: I might do!

ZAK: Go on then!

BIMLA: I might tell your Marcia. I might tell her how you broke your gun over somebody's head.

ZAK: And I'll tell your brother that you've been playing with rats, and how I told you he wanted you and you didn't go.

BIMLA: I am going. I'm going now. And when I come back that doll had better be mended, or else!

ZAK (*throwing the doll down*): Get lost!

BIMLA: Well, you broke it!

ZAK: I said I'm sorry. (*Pause.*)

BIMLA: I wouldn't really tell your sister on you.

ZAK: I wouldn't tell your brother on you.

BIMLA: I'll see you in a minute.

ZAK: Alright.

    BIMLA *exits.*

Scene Five: ZAK

ZAK *picks up the doll and the arm, sits down and prepares to replace the arm, talking to the doll as he does so. He replaces the arm, sits the doll on his knee, straightens its dress, etc.*

ZAK: There you are.

Scene Six: ZAK and STEPHEN

Enter STEPHEN *towards the end of the
above action. He looks at* ZAK *and the
doll.* ZAK *sees him, hides the doll behind
his back, then throws it to the ground
and gets up. He picks up his gun.*

STEPHEN: Where's Bimla?

ZAK: I don't know.

STEPHEN: Aren't you playing with her?

ZAK: No. I don't play with girls.

STEPHEN: What you doing with her doll
then?

ZAK: I found it. I was just going to
execute it. (ZAK *jumps over the wall.*)
Do you play with Bimla then? Do you
play babies and that?

STEPHEN: No. I just met her that's all.

ZAK (*swinging from the door frame*):
You from the new estate?

STEPHEN: We've just moved. From
Dewsbury.

ZAK: Who do you support?

STEPHEN: Eh?

ZAK: Football team?

STEPHEN: Who do you support?

ZAK: Liverpool.

STEPHEN: Yeah, that's who I support.

ZAK: Why?

STEPHEN: Why do you support them?

ZAK: 'Cos they're the best.

STEPHEN: That's why I support them.

ZAK: Who was their top-goal scorer last
season? (*Pause.* STEPHEN *pretends
to think.*) Bruce Grobbelar, wasn't
it?

STEPHEN: Yeah, that's right.

ZAK: He didn't score any! He's the
rotten goal-keeper.

STEPHEN: Who was it then?

ZAK: Ian Rush.

STEPHEN: Oh yeah, I got mixed up.

ZAK: You didn't know.

STEPHEN: I did. I bet you don't know
what that's called.

ZAK: Course I do.

STEPHEN: What?

ZAK: White stuff.

STEPHEN: It's called 'expanded
polystyrene' and it's deceptively
strong.

ZAK: So?

STEPHEN: You didn't know.

ZAK: So?

STEPHEN: Nothing.

ZAK: Clever clogs. Do you want to fight?

STEPHEN: No, I can't. I've gotta go
home now.

ZAK: You've got to fight me first.

STEPHEN: I'm not allowed. I broke my
leg in three places . . . in PE . . . and I
had to have a metal pin in it, so I
can't go near magnets.

ZAK: So?

STEPHEN: It's not healed up yet.

ZAK: I broke my leg. There. My sister
pushed me off a bus.

STEPHEN: My sister pushed me out of a
tree once.

ZAK: How old is she?

STEPHEN: Eleven. How old's yours?

ZAK: Fourteen. They're rotten, aren't
they?

STEPHEN: Yeah.

ZAK: Girls.

STEPHEN (*almost inaudible*): Yeah.

ZAK: Let's have a look at yours then?

STEPHEN: She's out playing somewhere.

ZAK: Not your sister dafthead, your leg.

STEPHEN: No, it's horrible.

ZAK: You're a liar.

STEPHEN: I'm not.

ZAK: I tell lies. I'm the best liar in our street. I'm the best liar in our school. Let's wrestle.

STEPHEN: No.

ZAK: I won't hurt you.

STEPHEN: I can't. If I get my clothes mucky, my mam'll kill me. I could show you a hold though.

ZAK: Alright.

STEPHEN: We have to get in a space. (ZAK *does as* STEPHEN *says.*) Turn round. It's called a full nelson. I put my hands here . . . and I lift you like this . . . I'll put you down now, shall I? . . . I'm putting you down . . . (ZAK *falls to the ground and lies still.*) Stop kidding about . . . I know you're kidding, so you might as well get up. I didn't mean to, honest. (*Retreats.*) I have to go home now . . . (ZAK *giggles.*) Are you laughing? You're laughing, aren't you?

ZAK (*bursting out laughing*): Yeah. I had you worried, didn't I?

STEPHEN: Yeah.

ZAK: It's a good hold though. What's your name?

STEPHEN: Stephen.

ZAK: Stephen! That's a sissy name. I'll call you Steve. I'm Zak.

STEPHEN: Are you playing?

ZAK: Yeah.

STEPHEN: Castles.

ZAK: Castles?

STEPHEN: Yeah. I built a castle before, and I was king of it. These are the battlements, and this is the drawbridge and this could be the moat, etc.

ZAK: And you're the king?

STEPHEN: Yeah. Well it is my castle.

ZAK: What am I then?

STEPHEN: You could be the dirty rascal.

ZAK: Alright. And I'll have the gun.

STEPHEN: But you've got to do what the king tells you.

ZAK: Why?

STEPHEN: 'Cos you have.

ZAK: Why?

STEPHEN: It's like a teacher, or your mam and dad. You have to do what they say, don't you.

ZAK: No.

STEPHEN: You do, or you get into trouble, 'cos they're bigger than you aren't they? They can hit you and stuff, and keep you in. They could starve you to death if they wanted to.

ZAK: So?

STEPHEN: It's the same with kings. They're dead rich and that, and everybody has to do what they're told, or they get thrown in dungeons and have their hands chopped off.

ZAK: Only if they get caught.

STEPHEN: Well, yeah.

ZAK: Right. You're the king then.

STEPHEN: Right. And you have to call me 'Your Majesty'. And I'm in my throne room and you come to me. (*Pause.* ZAK *stands looking at* STEPHEN.) Have you come?

ZAK: Yeah.

STEPHEN: Well kneel down then. (ZAK *does so.*) What is it, dirty rascal?

ZAK: *I* don't know.

STEPHEN: Make summat up. Do you have a message, dirty rascal?

ZAK: Yeah. Your Majesty. There's a load of men out here with guns.

STEPHEN: What do they want?

ZAK: They're cheesed off, 'cos they're starving to death, and you've got all the money.

STEPHEN: Who are they? Are they peasants?

ZAK: They're my mates. (*Shoots* STEPHEN.) You're dead! *Pause.*

STEPHEN: You wouldn't do that.

ZAK: I have.

STEPHEN: You'd be dead then, 'cos my soldiers'd shoot you.

ZAK: No they wouldn't, 'cos they're cheesed off as well. They're all on my side.

STEPHEN: Who's on my side then?

ZAK: I don't know.

STEPHEN: Other rich people, powerful people.

ZAK: There's only a handful of them though and there's millions of us dirty rascals. Come on, I've shot you.

STEPHEN: Well?

ZAK: So you gotta die. (STEPHEN *dies.*) Serves you right.

STEPHEN: Eh, I know, we're both dirty rascals, and this is our castle.

ZAK: Yeah. (*Picks up doll.*) And we've captured this princess and we're going to execute her. (*Props the doll up.*)

STEPHEN: Yeah.

ZAK: Here you are, Steve. (*Giving the gun.*) You have a go with it.

STEPHEN *takes the gun. Pause. He looks at the gun, then the doll.*

Scene Seven: STEPHEN, ZAK and BIMLA

Enter BIMLA *unnoticed.*

ZAK (*to* STEPHEN): Go on then. Shoot her. (STEPHEN *points the gun.*)

BIMLA: What are you doing?

STEPHEN: Just playing.

BIMLA: What you playing?

STEPHEN: King of the castle and dirty rascals.

BIMLA: Can I play? (STEPHEN *looks at*

ZAK, ZAK *looks from* STEPHEN *to* BIMLA, *then looks away.*)

ZAK: No.

BIMLA: Why not? . . . Why not, Stephen?

ZAK: 'Cos we don't play with girls, do we Steve?

BIMLA: Since when? (*To* STEPHEN.) I'll have my book back then.

STEPHEN: I left it at home. (ZAK *grabs the doll.*)

BIMLA (*holding out her hand for it*): Give us it.

ZAK: No, we're holding it hostage, aren't we Steve? (*To* STEPHEN.) Here, catch. (*Throws the doll to* STEPHEN.) Bimla in the middle. (*The three change positions.*) Here, throw it to me. Quick. (STEPHEN *gives the doll to* BIMLA.) What you give it to her for? Spoil sport! (BIMLA *slaps* ZAK *on the shoulder.*) Watch it!

BIMLA: You're a bully, you are!

ZAK: It's only a bit of fun, and I mended it for you.

BIMLA: Come on Stephen, let's go to my house and watch the video.

STEPHEN: Can't we all play together?

ZAK (*shrugs*): If you want.

BIMLA: I don't want to.

STEPHEN: Go on.

BIMLA: Alright.

ZAK: You're the dirty rascal Steve, 'cos you've got the gun, and I'm the king.

BIMLA: I'm the queen then.

ZAK: Yeah. And there's a war and me and the army have to defend the castle.

STEPHEN: Yeah. To the battlements. (*All three rush to the wall and start shooting.*)

ZAK: Bimla! You can't do it.

BIMLA: I can.

ZAK: No. You've got to get our dinner ready and look after the baby.

BIMLA: Stephen can do that.

ZAK: Don't be daft. Steve's the army, he's got the gun.

BIMLA: But we need the best fighters, don't we, or we'll all be doomed. And I'm a much better fighter than Stephen.

STEPHEN: You have to do what the king says though, Bimla.

BIMLA: Not if he's stupid.

STEPHEN: Kings aren't stupid though, they're dead clever.

BIMLA: Zak Taylor shouldn't be king then. He's thick.

ZAK: Who says?

BIMLA: Ask anybody. Ask our teacher.

ZAK: I'm not!

BIMLA: What are you on the bottom table for then? And he's got no manners.

ZAK: At least I'm not posh like you.

BIMLA: Kings are posh though, aren't they?

ZAK: So?

BIMLA: So I should be the king.

STEPHEN: Kings aren't girls though.

BIMLA: Queen then. But I'm the boss.

ZAK: Girls can't be boss.

BIMLA: They can.

ZAK: They can't.

BIMLA: Who's the boss of this country then?

ZAK: It's not the queen, is it Steve?

STEPHEN: No, it's the Prime Minister.

BIMLA: And who's the Prime Minister? (ZAK *looks at* STEPHEN.)

STEPHEN: Margaret Thatcher.

BIMLA: And *her* mum and dad had a shop.

ZAK: Alright, you're King Margaret Thatcher, and me and Steve are dirty rascals.

STEPHEN: Yeah.

BIMLA: And these sweets are the wages. Dirty Rascal Stephen, you stop at home and make the dinners and look after Princess Veronica, and if you do a good job, I'll give you a sweet. Dirty Rascal Zak, you're the best fighter, so you can guard the castle, and if you do a good job, you get two sweets.

STEPHEN: That's not fair.

ZAK: Course it is.

STEPHEN: Why?

ZAK: 'Cos I do a hard job, don't I, you just make the dinners and look after the baby.

STEPHEN: That's a hard job.

ZAK: People don't get paid for it though.

STEPHEN: They should do.

BIMLA: You do, you're getting a sweet.

STEPHEN: But he's getting two.

ZAK: I do the fighting. Fighting's more important.

STEPHEN: No it isn't!

BIMLA: If you don't stop arguing, Stephen, you won't get anything.

STEPHEN *is silent.* ZAK *holds his hand out for the gun.* STEPHEN *gives it to him and begins to organise Veronica and the kitchen.*

ZAK (*from the 'battlements'*): Eh, Your Majesty, there's a load of men out here with guns.

BIMLA: What do they want?

ZAK: It's the peasants and they're cheesed off 'cos you've got all the money.

BIMLA: No it's not. Look. It's them skinheads off the new estate coming to attack us.

ZAK: Yeah.

BIMLA: To the battlements! (ZAK *and* BIMLA *shoot.*) They're climbing up the walls! (*Shooting.*) Look out, Dirty Rascal. (*Gun noise.*) Stephen, come quick, Zak's been shot. (ZAK *writhes in agony.*)

STEPHEN: I'll take him to the hospital.

ZAK: It's alright, it only grazed me.

BIMLA: We're running out of bullets. Quick, Dirty Rascal, give me your gun.

ZAK: I'm alright now.

BIMLA: He's not, is he Doctor Stephen?

STEPHEN: No. He's got to go to the hospital. He's very badly wounded.

ZAK: I'm not.

BIMLA: I'm King Margaret Thatcher and I'm ordering you to go to the hospital. So you have to.

ZAK: No, I don't. 'Cos the war's made you crackers and I have to shoot you. (*Shoots.*)

BIMLA: You've got no bullets.

ZAK: I had one left.

BIMLA: And it hit my bullet-proof vest, bounced back and killed you! Stone dead! Dirty Rascal Stephen, we've won the war now, and you've done such a good job, I'm giving you two sweets. (*She does so.*)

STEPHEN: Thank you, Your Majesty.

ZAK: What about me?

BIMLA: You're dead.

ZAK: I was only badly wounded.

BIMLA: What do you think Doctor Stephen? Is this traitor, who just tried to shoot me with his last bullet, dead or just very very badly wounded?

STEPHEN: I'm not sure.

BIMLA: Give him an injection then, with poison in it, to make sure. (STEPHEN *does so.*) And now you are dead!

ZAK: But my ghost comes back, and smashes your rotten castle to bits!

ZAK *begins to destroy the castle.*

STEPHEN: Stop it! (ZAK *ignores him till he runs out of steam.*) It took me ages to build that.

ZAK: It's her fault. I told you we shouldn't play with girls. They always spoil things.

BIMLA: Come on Stephen, let's play somewhere else.

ZAK: She thinks you'll go and play with her 'cos she's got sweets. But sweets aren't everything, are they Steve?

STEPHEN: No.

ZAK: See! No one wants to play with you Bimla Seth, 'cos you're stuck up and bossy!

BIMLA: You stop with him Stephen and he'll only bully you.

ZAK: I won't.

BIMLA: He will. Zak Taylor broke his rifle today and I know how he did it. My brother saw him.

ZAK: So?

BIMLA: He hit your sister Maureen over the head with it.

STEPHEN: Did you?

ZAK: Yeah.

BIMLA: See, and he thinks it's funny.

STEPHEN: Do you?

ZAK: Yeah.

BIMLA: Smack him one Stephen.

ZAK: Yeah, come on Steve.

STEPHEN: No.

BIMLA: I'll help you. Come on, let's get him.

STEPHEN: I don't want to. I don't like fighting.

ZAK: His mam won't let him. In case he gets his dress mucky. Eh, Steve?

STEPHEN: My name's Stephen. Why did you hit my sister?

ZAK: 'Cos she was calling me names.

STEPHEN: Calling names is nothing.

ZAK: It depends what they call you.

BIMLA: I bet she called him a thicko . . .

STEPHEN: What did she call you?

ZAK: She called me a wog.

STEPHEN: Well you are one, aren't you?

ZAK: What?

STEPHEN: He is, isn't he, Bimla?

BIMLA: What?

STEPHEN: A wog. It just means you're coloured, that's all.

ZAK: And what's she, then?

STEPHEN: Bimla. She's a Paki.

BIMLA: I'm gonna smack you, Stephen.

STEPHEN: Why? It just means you're from Pakistan . . .

BIMLA: But I'm not.

STEPHEN: That you're the colour of people from Pakistan . . .

BIMLA: It does heck. It means the same as wog. If someone calls you a wog or a Paki they mean they think you're rubbish, 'cos you're not white.

STEPHEN: They don't. They just mean you're coloured, that's all.

BIMLA: You're coloured.

STEPHEN: I'm not.

BIMLA: You are. You're pink.

ZAK: He's yellow more like.

STEPHEN: I'm not coloured. I'm normal.

BIMLA: So am I!

ZAK: You're the one who's rubbish 'cos you're a rotten sissy.

STEPHEN: Yeah. I am a sissy, so what. It don't mean you're better than me.

ZAK: And I'm black, so what?

BIMLA: And I'm Indian, so what?

ZAK: It don't mean you're better than us.

STEPHEN: I'm going home.

ZAK: Me too.

BIMLA: I am. (*Pause.*)

STEPHEN: Do you know what our Maureen calls me when I get her mad?

ZAK: What?

STEPHEN: Andrex. It's toilet paper. She put me head down the toilet once and flushed it. And you know what I did?

ZAK: What?

STEPHEN: I went 'blub, blub, blub, blub'. (*He laughs.*)

ZAK: You're a nutcase.

BIMLA *laughs.* ZAK *laughs. They go round going 'blub, blub' etc. Pause.*

BIMLA: Eh, I know, we're all a gang and this is our secret den.

STEPHEN: Yeah.

ZAK: Yeah.

BIMLA: And we've got our magic stone and we keep it in our secret hole, over there, that only we know about.

STEPHEN (*to* ZAK): It's a rat hole.

ZAK: I know.

BIMLA: It's not really. I was just kidding you. (*Laughs, others join in.* STEPHEN *gets the ammonite.*)

STEPHEN: And we share everything. (*He puts the ammonite in the middle.*)

ZAK: Alright. (*Puts his gun in the middle.*)

BIMLA: Yeah. (*Puts her doll and then the sweets in the middle.*) And nobody's better than anybody else. And we all stick up for each other.

STEPHEN: Yeah.

ZAK: Yeah.

STEPHEN: What are we called?

BIMLA: Yeah, we have to have a secret name.

ZAK: The kings . . .

BIMLA: The magic stone gang . . .

STEPHEN: The dirty rascals!

BIMLA: The dirty rascals?

STEPHEN: That's what we are really, we're all dirty rascals.

ZAK: Yeah.

BIMLA: Yeah.

ZAK: Who's boss?

BIMLA: Me, 'cos I'm the cleverest.

ZAK: But I'm the toughest.

STEPHEN: We don't have a boss.

ZAK: We have to have a boss.

STEPHEN: Why? We're all dirty rascals, right? And we share everything, and nobody's better than anybody else, right? And we all stick up for each other, right? So we don't have a boss, right? (BIMLA *nods.*)

ZAK: Alright.

STEPHEN (*picks up the ammonite*): We've all got to tell a secret . . .

BIMLA: You first.

STEPHEN: You know I broke my leg in three places . . . I didn't. It was a lad at school called Merve Dean. (*He gives the ammonite to* ZAK.)

ZAK: You know I hit your sister over the head with me gun . . . after that she bashed me up.

BIMLA: And you cried, didn't you?

ZAK: Yeah. (*Passes the stone to* BIMLA.)

BIMLA: I used to be rotten at tests. But now I'm dead good at them. D'you know why? . . . I copy off David Dunk. (BIMLA *replaces the stone, then picks it up again.*) When I grow up I'm going to be a doctor, and go to India for all my holidays. (*Passes stone to* STEPHEN.)

STEPHEN: When I grow up I'm going to be a gasman like me dad. Or I might be a computer scientist. (*Passes it to* ZAK.)

ZAK: When I grow up I'm going to be rich. (*They laugh.*)

STEPHEN: But what're you going to do?

ZAK: I don't know. (*More laughter.*)

BIMLA: Now we have to swear on the magic stone that we'll never tell. I swear. (*Passes stone to* STEPHEN.)

STEPHEN: I swear. (*To* ZAK.)

ZAK: I swear. (*Pause.*)

BIMLA: I've got to go for my tea now.

ZAK: Me too.

STEPHEN: And me, but we have to keep all our stuff here.

They hide their things.

BIMLA: See you after tea then.

STEPHEN: Yeah, see you.

ZAK: See you.

They exit.

Dirty Rascals

The Workshop: We placed in the play a complex web of symbol, through which the children in the play understand their world — the games, the toys, the place in which they play. With the aid of these we could explore almost anything that the class suggested in the workshop. These things were varied and not always the things which preoccupied the characters.

In the workshop children might be much more concerned with exploring questions such as, 'Why would you stick up for one person and not another?'; 'What is a real friend?'; 'Are we all the same?'; 'Are we all different?'; 'Should you do what your parents tell you?' We welcomed this. At every stage of the day the children were encouraged to express their own opinions and the programme was devised in order to address their *real* concerns.

The workshop took many directions but we used two basic starting points:

Version One:
We enrolled the class as 'dirty rascals' with the actors as the characters from the play. To do this we used the ammonite and the idea of a den. We built a den with the class in the school hall, using whatever was available — chairs, tables, benches etc. At this point one of the characters would reveal that they could not come to play anymore and would leave the gang. The class would then set out to find out why this had happened. It is important to stress that we had no pre-set narrative in our minds, no story for the children to follow. We allowed the class to decide what they would like to explore next, and often how they would like to do it.

Version Two:
This format kept a company member in the teacher role throughout. The other two actors would begin an improvisation as characters from the play, using the end of the play (i.e. returning after tea) as the starting point. They would improvise a game and out of this a conflict would grow, usually over leaving the den and going out into the outside world. At a high point of conflict the company member in the teacher 'role' would freeze the action and ask the children what they would like to happen next.

In both versions of the workshop we used a wide variety of techniques — role play, discussion, narrative; we would play out suggestions, take on other characters as needed, enact flashbacks and offer our own opinions as actors if asked.

PEACEMAKER

Written by David Holman

A Programme For 5-8 Years Old

Peacemaker and Under Exposure

The two plays in this volume which originated at Theatre Centre represent part of a very large repertoire of some nearly fifty new plays and programmes produced by the company in the last ten years. All of those pieces were created by various forms of collective team-work and these two are no exception. The process has been a fascinating one for all the company and also highly successful.

By collective team-work, I do not mean group-devising in the traditional TIE sense where the whole of a team may plan, discuss, improvise and ultimately write a script, though a minority of Theatre Centre scripts have been produced in this way. All of our scripts are the result of collective team-work, that is group discussion and thinking on themes, issues, content etc. Writers have usually worked in close co-operation with one or two people in the company, usually the director and/or designer of the piece, throughout the process.

Many of the scripts produced have been performed by other companies at home and abroad. In recent years, Theatre Centre has been invited to tour its work in other countries, giving writers, directors, and designers who have worked with the team the opportunity to work with theatre organisations all over the (mainly English-speaking) world. If it could be argued in 1976 that there was a dearth of good playable scripts for young people in this country, that certainly is far from the case today. Hopefully Theatre Centre can claim some responsibility for that healthy state of affairs.

When the new team working at Theatre Centre in 1976 started the process of searching out new writers, scripts and ways of working, we were greatly helped by the fact that the Arts Council was creating new writing schemes and looking for established companies to utilise them. As a result, companies like Theatre Centre, who engaged whole-heartedly with the schemes, were able to increase their capacity to commission without putting any great strain on their central budgets. The company commissioned several writers in the first few years, but it was not until 1978 that we employed a resident writer, and the two scripts in this volume were written by the two writers, David Holman and Lisa Evans, who were resident successively with the company between 1979 and 1984.

It was an exciting time. The company had been growing in confidence throughout the late 1970s, retaining a 'children's theatre' form. Into this was introduced the social, educational and political issues and themes which new members, mainly from experienced TIE backgrounds, wished to pursue and develop. The company was touring on a national basis and carrying out innovatory experiments in the London boroughs of Islington and Hackney. The company had also undergone the process of revolutionising its internal organisational process. By 1981 this had led to an equal wage structure, the creation of stronger and more central roles for women in the work, positive action to become a multi-racial company, and the formation of a central policy-making body, 'The Base Company', to orchestrate decisions which had originally been taken by the director alone. Outside greater London, the company was touring mainly rural conservative areas, yet had managed to explore some fairly controversial issues: gender roles, Third World military dictatorship, imperialism, industrial and agricultural pollution. I believe the main reason for this was that, throughout the whole period, the company never lost sight of the need to create an increasingly higher standard of theatrical presentation with skilled writers, directors, designers and performers, and therefore any challenge could not be cloaked in artistic or educational terms, but would have to be overtly political.

In 1982 the company decided to tackle its most controversial topic yet, the 'Peace Theme', presenting Peace plays to the whole age range within schools for at least a year. This was to lead to probably our most difficult and successful year up until that time, to five very different and highly accomplished scripts, to the company being roundly condemned in the national media by a senior Conservative government minister, Norman Tebbit MP (without his having bothered to find out any details of the work), and to the company touring a play about cruise missiles around London at the same time as the issue was being centrally debated in a General Election (1983). It was an extraordinary time; the whole company worked with a commitment unparalleled up to that time and some extraordinary work emerged. The script of *Peacemaker* included in this volume was the end product of the work for five to eight year olds during this period, and its subsequent success would suggest that it was a little out of the ordinary and remains so.

The question of Peace Studies in school was then, and is still, a controversial one and a great deal of care and concern went into the planning of the Peace plays. We felt it important to avoid propaganda yet equally important to select material that would supply young people with information that provided an alternative to what was coming from the established media. This process resulted in a wide range of plays: *Red Letter Days* by Geoff Bullen, about international exchange between British and Soviet students; *Susumu's Story* by David Holman, about a family living in Hiroshima in World War II; *Bunkers* by Jamal Ali, a Caribbean musical about the end of the world; and *1983* by David Holman, a story about a relationship between an American pilot and an Englishwoman on a cruise-missile base. *ABC* by David Holman, a play about the literacy campaign mounted in post-revolutionary peacetime in Nicaragua was the final play produced directly on the Peace theme.

In the process of preparing all these scripts, we had to ask ourselves what were the essential elements in the material which were appropriate for the age range concerned, and in this respect we had the greatest difficulty with the five to eight year olds. Eventually we settled on the theme of 'conflict resolution'. This age group is constantly involved in some form of conflict, with parents, teachers, their peers, and there is no doubt that a great deal of unresolved conflict at this age can contribute to, and exacerbate, the more dangerous conflicts which as adults they may decide to engage in. So we searched for an image, a central conflict, and out of this the image of the wall, and the Red and Blue people, began to emerge.

The first meeting of two people from either side of an impenetrable wall, two people both greatly influenced by propaganda about 'the other side', seemed to have both the qualities of parable and concrete reality that we all felt this age group required. Whether one saw the wall as a 'Berlin' wall, a barrier between races, or simply any of the psychological barriers and prejudices that we all build, it seemed to speak to us on many different levels. The actual script went through several changes before arriving at the version in this volume, but the central story always remained the same, however differently it was framed by the different versions.

Why has *Peacemaker* been so successful since its inception? (There have been many national and international productions; Theatre Centre just toured yet another version of it in North America this year). The fact that it is simple, clear, tightly-written, humorous, entertaining, poignant, obviously helps, but that would be true of many of our scripts from the last ten years. What I feel is so special about *Peacemaker* is that it reduces to a simple concrete level much of what is normally presented through the media and through education in overcomplicated mystifying jargon. It is easy to teach from, non-moralistic, hopeful, yet not over-idealistic. It is a clear and simple answer to those who still argue that children under eight years old must remain in a protected cocoon and are incapable of understanding anything except escapist fantasy. I can think of no better product to introduce a young audience to the delights and challenges of a truly political theatre, which is what good TIE is all about.

By the time of Theatre Centre's first production of *Under Exposure* in March 1981, the company had developed further. We had a new resident writer, Lisa Evans, and had started to become a truly multi-racial company. Over two years, through a process of positive action, advertising, contacting drama schools, making links with Afro-Caribbean groups, visiting youth theatres etc., we had tapped previously neglected sources of young black talent in the theatre world. This led to our having a majority of black performers, a policy of integrated casting, and the ability to look at racial and cultural issues in a truly representative way. Other companies were to follow this lead, both in the TIE field and elsewhere. In addition, the previous year had seen the formation of a permanent all-women's company at Theatre Centre. This company issued a policy statement at the end of their first year which stated:

> The Women's Company at Theatre Centre came about as a statement of recognition: recognition of oppression in the lives of girls and women; recognition of inequality between the sexes at school, at work, at home and on the streets; and recognition of the need for positive action by women to do something about it.

At first our actions were guided by two outstanding concerns:
1. To create opportunities for women in a male-dominated profession by employing women as performers, administrators, writers, designers and directors.

2. To make an initiative toward anti-sexist education by developing the imagery and language of theatre from a female perspective in order to provide an affirmative experience for girls, and a subtly challenging experience for boys.

The plays produced by the Women's Company are a celebration of the quality of work which women can achieve. They are also an acknowledgement of the difficulties encountered on the way, and of the help we receive from Theatre Centre as a whole company and from our associates and from our audience.

Under Exposure was the fifth production which the Women's Company presented and probably the most instrumental in firmly establishing them on a nationally acclaimed basis. The play ran in various forms for over a year. Although it was initially conceived for 9-13 year olds, we eventually toured it for audiences of all ages in schools and theatres throughout the country, and it was specially chosen to open the Arts Council's 1984 conference on TIE at Warwick University.

Under Exposure was one of a number of plays written for Theatre Centre on an anti-racist theme, a theme which had evolved organically by examining 'peace' in a broader global context, with particular reference to the diverse cultural and racial backgrounds which were now informing the collective process from within the company. So the work was starting to take its inspiration now much more from the personal politics and experience of the company itself. Interestingly enough, the writers were also increasingly creating work from their own conceptions and motivations, and we were bringing freelance directors and designers into the company to challenge and support the next stage of our development.

The idea for the play came very much from Lisa Evans' desire, after extensive research, to write a play about the lives of women living in squatter camps in South Africa, demonstrating their strength and courage. Like most of our plays, it went through several drafts and restructuring in the rehearsal process.

The production of *Under Exposure* led to a consolidation of the Women's Company at Theatre Centre, and a project by the resident writer to create a resource file of potential women writers. Sadly, despite its popularity, there has only been one further production of the play since our own (Sheffield Crucible TIE, 1985), and another currently being planned at Theatre Foundry, Walsall. Does the challenge of an all women's show requiring four performers (three black and one white) celebrating three struggles in one (race, class, gender) still prove too great for British Theatre? I realise that for small permanent companies the racial casting may present problems but what about those companies who cast on a show-by-show basis?

Like *Peacemaker, Under Exposure*'s success derived from the fact that it was good, well-produced theatre, humorous, entertaining, joyous and sad, educational and still able to engage an audience of young people simply and clearly on a political level. Neither *Peacemaker* nor *Under Exposure* present easy answers to the questions they pose. The wall does not stay down. It has to be rebuilt because the forces which control us are still very strong. But a chink remains. Likewise, the squatters camp at Crossroads is still being destroyed today; the violence has become inevitably internecine, and slow, painful struggle for change in South Africa goes on. None the less, to the extent that theatre can support the struggle for social change in the world, both these plays will continue to act as powerful catalysts for thought, debate and, eventually, action.

David Johnston,
Director, Theatre Centre, 1976-1986

Peacemaker was first produced by Theatre Centre on 13 September 1982, with the following cast:

BLUEY   Winston Crooke
SIMP   Eileen George
FRANNY   Delmozene Morris
MR MAN   John O'Mahoney

Written by David Holman
Directed by Gwenda Hughes
Designed by Bill Mitchell

A wall between five and six feet high. When first seen, covered with a cloth. Audience in a half circle. Music introduction.
SIMP stands in front of the wall.

SIMP: Hello, we've come to tell you about our land. This is what we look like in the land of Red. Everything's red. Sad really. We haven't got any other colours. Mind you, it wasn't always like this. A long time ago in our land there were red people, yes, but blue people as well. Red people lived in the South and Blue people in the North. But they were always coming and going, going and coming, meeting each other. Because between North and South there was a bridge. With only room for one person to pass. So Red people come. . .

A red puppet appears over the top of the wall. Makes sound. Waves at the kids.

And Blue people come.

Blue puppet appears over the top of the wall. Makes different sound. Waves at the kids.

The two puppets march towards each other, comically singing.

And look at that. Reds and Blues getting along fine. But remember. The bridge is only wide enough for one person to cross at a time. So some days the Blue person goes back so that the Red can pass . . .

Blue puppet bows and allows red puppet to pass.

Next day the Red person goes back so that the Blue one can pass.

This is done.

This way everything is fine. In fact, the Blues and the Reds are really good friends. Then one day . . . Well, watch what happened . . .

The red and the blue puppets move towards each other as they have done before. Only this time neither is

prepared to give way. There are grunts, wild sounds, as they stand there next to each other. Then they both reach out and push each other. Then they tap each other with the sticks they carry. Then slowly a full-scale fight. Loud cries. Both puppets die.

Yes, there was a big big fight. And not just these two. I mean all the Blues came to fight . . .

A blue puppet rises roaring above the wall.

And all the Reds came to fight . . .

Red puppet up and roars. Cymbals and drums. They fight and roar.

Cracked heads. Split bones. Broken teeth. Grazed knees . . .

Puppets roar in pain. They cry.

The Reds were very angry. 'You started it!'

Red puppet accuses blue.

The Blues were very angry. 'No, you started it!'

Blue puppet accuses red.
SIMP approaches the puppets.

Shake hands?

Both puppets stand stiffly to sulky attention. Shake their heads.

Nobody would shake hands. No one would be friends.

Puppets grunt and disappear.

So what to do?

Music begins.

The only way anyone could think to stop the fighting was for the Reds never to meet a Blue, and for a Blue never to meet a Red ever again. So it was decided to build . . .

Another performer pulls at the cloth covering the wall. The wall is revealed.

A wall.

Discord within the music.
Music continues.

Right across the country. From East to West a huge high wall with Blues on one side and Reds on the other. And since that day no Red has ever met a Blue. All that happened many years ago but still nobody is supposed to go near the wall. But watch . . . because today . . .

A loud twirl of a rattle off stage and then MR MAN *comes on twirling his noisy rattle.*

MR MAN: Get away from the wall! Get away from the wall.

He checks his alarm clock which hangs at his belt.

It's nearly time! Twelve minutes to sunset. Get away from the wall.

And goes off, still rattling. FRANNY *comes on, breathless. She pants.*

FRANNY: Simp! Simp! (*To audience.*) Oh hello. I'm looking for my friend. She looks a bit like me. She's about my height. And she's probably got three rubber balls. She's learning how to juggle. That's why I'm here. I said I'd meet her here by the wall so I can help her learn to juggle. It's quiet because we're not supposed to be here by the wall. Have you seen her? Simp! Simp!

The rattle is heard over these shouts. Then MR MAN *re-enters.*

MR MAN: Oi!! It's Franny isn't it? Well young Franny, didn't you hear this??

FRANNY: What?

MR MAN: This! 'Get away from the wall.' I don't know why I bother sometimes. Do you know why I do all this? To save people like you from being eaten by those Blues from over the wall. Do you know what time it is? The sun's on its way down and the Blues start to cause all sorts of trouble when the sun goes down. You know

you're not supposed to be here. So go on. Hop it!

FRANNY *hops away.*

MR MAN: Oh yes very comical. Go on! Home.

FRANNY: I've got to wait. I'm meeting Simp. I've got to help her learn to juggle for the carnival tomorrow. Can't I just wait ten minutes? Please?

MR MAN *rechecks his alarm clock.*

MR MAN: Well ten minutes then. But not a moment longer. Here, what are you doing at the Carnival tomorrow?

FRANNY: Me? I'm doing a dance, me. This one.

FANNY *demonstrates her dance.*

MR MAN: Very good. I can't go to the Carnival myself.

FRANNY: Oh why? It's great the carnival!

MR MAN: Yes. (*Sadly.*) I know.

FRANNY: Why can't you come?

MR MAN: Someone's got to guard the wall, haven't they? It would be just like the Blues to come over the wall and wreck everything when everyone's enjoying themselves, at our Carnival.

FRANNY: Yes I suppose.

MR MAN: They're very evil, Blues.

FRANNY: So they say.

MR MAN: Very nasty altogether.

He swings his rattle as SIMP *enters bumping into* MR MAN. *His rattle falls.*

SIMP: Sorry Mister. (*To* FRANNY.) Sorry. Sorry I'm late.

MR MAN: Simp!

SIMP: Yes?

MR MAN: You have got . . .

MR MAN *checks his alarm clock.*

Let's see . . . nine minutes.

He rattles.

SIMP: What?

MR MAN: You've got nine minutes in which to practise your juggling.

MR MAN *exits rattling.*

SIMP: Ohhhhh.

FRANNY: Come on, Simp. Show us your juggling. We haven't got much time.

SIMP *gets out her juggling balls.*

SIMP: Alright. Here goes. Oh I've got to be good at the Carnival tomorrow. I don't think I will be though.

MR MAN (*off*): Eight minutes!

SIMP: Alright. (*To* FRANNY.) Is your dance ready?

FRANNY: Yes thank you. Now, come on.

SIMP: I've been practising.

Rattle from offstage.

SIMP: Alright! It's good this.

SIMP *goes into her juggling with just two balls. It is pathetic. She is just throwing two balls separately into the air. She finishes.*

What do you think?

FRANNY *looks as if she doesn't know what to say about the pathetic display.* MR MAN *returns.*

MR MAN: You don't know nothing do you?

SIMP: What?

MR MAN: There are rules you know. There are rules about this wall and there are rules about juggling. And the first rule of juggling is that three balls are required. Not one ball, not two balls, but three balls.

SIMP: I haven't got three balls.

MR MAN: Well you'd better go and get another one hadn't you?

SIMP: Yes.

MR MAN: Yes. And you've only got six minutes to do it in!

FRANNY: Run Simp! Get another ball.

SIMP: I'm running.

SIMP *runs off.*

MR MAN (*watching her go*): Some people. In a million years that Simp will never juggle. Not in a million years. I don't know why you bother teaching her.

FRANNY: I have to try. It's for the Carnival.

MR MAN: The Carnival or not it's time to come away from that wall.

FRANNY: Why? There's nobody there. I can't hear anything.

MR MAN: When the Blues come after you you don't hear anything, young Franny.

FRANNY: No?

MR MAN: No. Not at first.

FRANNY: Have you seen one then? No, nobody has. Bet you haven't.

MR MAN: Oh haven't I? Can you keep a secret?

FRANNY: Yes.

MR MAN: Sure?

FRANNY: Yes.

MR MAN: Alright, sit down there and I'll tell you of my near fatal brush with . . . a Blue. Two weeks ago I'd cleared everyone away from the wall with my rattle. 'Get away from the wall.' Sun was going down but Ohhhhhh I'd got this lovely piece of redberry pie. And I was hungry. So I think to myself, well, just take a minute, sit by the wall, very quiet, eat my pie.

FRANNY: So?

MR MAN: So? It's the very biggest mistake I ever made in my life!

FRANNY: So?

MR MAN: So you're lucky I'm here alive today.

FRANNY: Really?

MR MAN: I went over to the wall. Stood here.

*He points to a section of wall. Then to
a foot further along the wall.*

I tell a lie. Here. Suddenly I felt this
something on my *right* shoulder.

FRANNY (*scared*): Ahhhhhhh.

MR MAN: That's just what I said. And
then there's this something on my
left shoulder. A cold grip! I look. A
huge hairy horrible blue claw. And
then *this* side. Another huge hairy
horrible blue claw.

FRANNY: Did you run?

MR MAN: Run? Couldn't run. I was
clamped. I look up and there's this
face with a mouth like a tunnel and
eyes like burning coal. Never seen
anything so horrible in my life. Then
suddenly there's this grunt and the
Blue lets go. Didn't stop to think. I
ran. Looked back. And what do you
think I saw?

FRANNY: What?

MR MAN: Nothing. And then slowly . . .
this horrible horrible laugh.

*SIMP has come on with a third rubber
ball. She is showing this to the kids.
SIMP laughs.* MR MAN *hasn't seen her
come on.* SIMP *is to* MR MAN's *right.
He looks over his left shoulder.*

MR MAN (*scared*): It was just like that.

Then SIMP *taps on* MR MAN's *right
shoulder.* MR MAN *jumps in the air
and lands in* FRANNY's *arms. Slowly
he looks around and sees that it is*
SIMP *who has laughed.*

FRANNY: Simp!

SIMP (*to* MR MAN): I got the other ball.
What are you doing up there?

MR MAN (*getting down ungraciously*):
You!!!

SIMP: What?

MR MAN: You little creep! Creeping up
on people!

SIMP: Me? I thought . . .

MR MAN: You may have thought what
you like. I'm sure you did.

SIMP (*holding up balls*): I'm ready.

MR MAN: Are you?

SIMP: I've got the other ball.

SIMP holds out three balls.

MR MAN: Pity. Because your time is up.

He takes the three balls from her.

And your juggling is up too.

FRANNY: No. It's not her fault. No!

MR MAN *approaches the wall to
throw them over.*

MR MAN: Creeping up behind.

Throws one over.

Two.

Throws second ball.

Three.

Throws third ball.

So nerrrr!

Pause. SIMP *head in hand. A big groan
from behind the wall.*

*Panic in the red ranks.
All moan.*

ALL: Ohhhhhhhhhhh.

MR MAN: The BLUES!!! Help! The
Blues are coming. Prepare to die.
Franny, go over there and panic. Man
the lifeboats. Save yourselves! Help!

FRANNY: The Blues.

*They run about. Getting in each
other's way.* SIMP *has stayed where
she is, hands over her ears.
Another groan from over the wall.*
FRANNY *and* MR MAN *run off.*
SIMP *is frozen in horror.
Pause.
Then one blue hand appears on
top of the wall. Then another blue
hand appears on the wall. It holds
a red ball. It drops the red ball.
It rolls to* SIMP. *Music accompaniment*
SIMP *slowly picks up the ball.*

Whoever is behind the wall throws a red ball in the air three times.

SIMP *watches.*

The red ball is thrown in the air another three times. We still haven't seen who is doing the throwing.

SIMP *creeps forward. Then starts back.*

The red ball is thrown in the air another three times.

SIMP *throws one ball in the air. This is replied to from behind the wall. (One ball.)*

SIMP *throws up her ball twice. Repeated from behind wall.*

SIMP *throws ball up three times. No reply. Silence.*

Then from behind wall a ball is thrown up at one end of the wall. Swiftly followed by a ball at the other end of the wall. (Are there two Blues behind the wall?)

SIMP *doesn't reply. She looks at her one ball. It is not enough to reply.*

From behind the wall two balls thrown in the air at the same time.

SIMP *angrily throws her one ball into the air.*

A blue hand thumps down on top of the wall. Another red ball is dropped over. SIMP *picks it up.*

She throws two balls in the air, one after the other.

Then she throws two balls up separately. And repeats. She is pleased.

Behind wall two balls are thrown together (once). The balls are now blue.

Music.

SIMP *is despondent. She can't do this.*

From behind the wall the move is repeated.

SIMP *tries to copy but fails. She bursts into tears.*

Pause.

A blue handkerchief is laid on the wall.

Cymbal.

SIMP *moves towards it slowly and takes it. She blows nose once.*

Blue hand makes sign of 'two.' She blows her nose again. (These are both accompanied by a hooter.)

Blue hand makes sign of 'two'. She (Finger and thumb in a circle.)

Pause.

Then blue hand comes over top of wall searching for handkerchief.

SIMP *places handkerchief where the blue hand has been.*

Hand comes on top of wall at different place.

This is repeated at various points on the top of the wall five times.

Then SIMP *puts the handkerchief down for the seventh time just as the blue hand is coming over the wall. They touch. Both leap back in fright.*

SIMP *runs away from the wall.*

Pause.

SIMP *creeps back to the wall. Tries to see over. She can't. She gets a box. Slowly she climbs on box. At the same moment the Blue's head comes over the wall. They look at each other.*

BOTH: Ahhhhhhhhhhhhhh.

SIMP *goes down to her knees on the box. Then slowly raises herself up and moves from wall.*

BLUEY *slowly reappears over the wall. He takes off his blue top hat and places it on the wall.*

BLUEY: Excuse me. Is this your ball?

He holds it out to her. Very slowly she comes to take it from him.

BLUEY: Can I have my handkerchief back please?

SIMP *nods and slowly brings it to him at the wall and then retreats.*

BLUEY: Are you a Red?

SIMP: Yes. Are you a Blue?

BLUEY: Yes.

SIMP: Are you going to eat me then?

BLUEY: No. Why should I?

SIMP: That's what Blues do. Everyone says.

BLUEY: Well we *don't*. Are you going to eat me then?

SIMP: No. Why?

BLUEY: Well that's what Reds do. Everyone says.

SIMP (*offended*): Well we *don't*!

BLUEY: That's alright then.

BLUEY *does a big blue hello. This is a strange gesture with his hand.* SIMP *is startled. She hasn't seen anything like this before.*

SIMP: What did you do that for?

BLUEY: It means 'hello' or 'I like you' or 'nice weather'.

SIMP: Is that how you say 'hello'?

BLUEY: Yes.

He repeats it.

BLUEY: Hello!

SIMP (*copying him*): Hello. What's your name?

BLUEY: Bluey. What's yours?

SIMP: Simp.

BLUEY: Simp? Simp?

SIMP: What's wrong with that?

BLUEY: Oh nothing.

SIMP (*doing his hello gesture*): Hello Bluey.

BLUEY (*repeating his gesture*): Hello Simp.

They repeat until it becomes continuous. SIMP *laughing.*

BLUEY: Hey Simp. Why were you crying?

SIMP: My juggling. I can't juggle.

She checks that no one is listening.

I'm not supposed to tell you but we've got this Carnival tomorrow. I'm the juggler but I'm hopeless.

BLUEY: Do you have Carnivals?

SIMP: Yes we have lovely Red Carnivals.

BLUEY: We have beautiful Blue Carnivals and I sometimes juggle at them.

SIMP: You're a juggler?

BLUEY: Yes I'm one of the best jugglers.

SIMP: Oh hey . . .

BLUEY: What?

SIMP: Could you . . .?

BLUEY: What?

SIMP: Could you teach me to juggle?

BLUEY: I could. But you'd have to teach *me* something.

SIMP: Yes.

BLUEY: I've got to go dance tonight. And I can't dance.

SIMP: Don't worry. I'll teach you to dance. If you teach me to juggle.

BOTH: Great!

Pause. Then SIMP *bursts into tears.*

BLUEY: What's the matter? (*Pause.*) What's the matter Simp?

SIMP: I just remembered.

BLUEY: What?

SIMP: I can't dance.

BLUEY: Ohhh.

SIMP: I'm worse at dancing than I am at juggling.

BLUEY: Pity. I fancy dancing.

SIMP: Now you won't teach me to juggle.

She cries again.

BLUEY: Yes I will. But only if you stop

crying. Now blow your nose. Come on. Blow your nose.

She does so. Hooter accompaniment.

BLUEY (*offering blue balls*): That's better. Now take these. They're bigger.

SIMP *takes the balls.*
Then a shout from offstage..

FRANNY (*off*): Simp!!!

BLUEY (*scared*): What's that?

FRANNY (*off*): Simp!!

SIMP: Oh no. It's Franny the Dancer. And she'll be frightened. Quick. Hide!

BLUEY *hides. Then comes back over wall again.*

BLUEY: She's a dancer?

SIMP: Yes. Get down!

BLUEY: Ask her to teach me.

SIMP: What?

BLUEY: Ask her to teach me to dance.

SIMP: Alright. I'll try. Now get down!

BLUEY *is now hidden.*

Your hat!!

BLUEY'*s hand retrieves the blue hat from the wall.*

Your handkerchief!

Handkerchief is retrieved. SIMP hides her blue juggling balls in her costume. She sits on the box by the wall. FRANNY enters, scared. She looks around wide-eyed.

FRANNY (*whispering*): Are you alright?

SIMP *nods.*

What happened?

SIMP *shrugs.*

Was it a Blue?

SIMP *nods her head and shakes it.*

Come on. Let's get out of here.

She grabs SIMP and pulls.

SIMP: Emmm. Franny? Suppose . . . well . . . suppose I knew someone who

really wanted to dance.

FRANNY (*still pulling*): Come on! What? Dance?

SIMP: Well would you be willing to . . . you know . . . teach them?

FRANNY: I might. Now come on.

SIMP: Yes but suppose . . . I mean just suppose . . . this person who wanted to learn to dance . . . just suppose that person, yes?

FRANNY: Yes.

SIMP: Well. Was a Blue?

FRANNY: A Blue?

SIMP: Well yes kind of Blue.

FRANNY: A Blue???

SIMP: He's a very nice Blue.

FRANNY: You want me to teach a Blue to dance?

SIMP: Shhhh. I know what people say but it's not true. Cross my heart.

SIMP *lets go of FRANNY.*
FRANNY *runs. SIMP grabs her.*

SIMP: I've been talking to him. (*To audience.*) We're really good friends aren't we? (*To FRANNY.*) If I ask him to come out you can see for yourself. Trust me.

SIMP *lets go of FRANNY.*
FRANNY *stays.*
SIMP *goes to the wall and whispers.*

SIMP: Bluey?

BLUEY (*unseen and hiding*): Yes.

SIMP: Bluey, Franny's here and she could teach you to dance. Would you like her to?

BLUEY: No I don't think so. I'm a little bit scared.

SIMP: But she's a bit scared too.

BLUEY: Who of?

SIMP: You.

BLUEY: Oh.

And very slowly BLUEY *appears over the top of the wall.*
SIMP *prompts him by doing his hello gesture.*
BLUEY *does it to* FRANNY.
FRANNY *does a jump back, scared.*

SIMP: No, that's just his way of saying 'hello'. Do it back to him.

BLUEY *repeats gesture.*

BLUEY: Hello.

FRANNY (*doing gesture*): Hello.

Both smile.

BLUEY (*indicating himself*): I'm Bluey.

FRANNY (*indicating herself*): I'm Franny.

SIMP: I'm Simp.

They all laugh.

Bluey, Franny can teach you to dance, can't you Franny?

FRANNY *nods.*

He's going to teach me to juggle.

FRANNY: Really?

SIMP: Yes. Right. Juggling!

BLUEY: Juggling!

SIMP: You do it and I'll copy.

BLUEY: OK. But I'll have to get down to show you.

BLUEY *disappears behind the wall. They wait and watch. Nothing happens.*

SIMP: Are you doing it?

BLUEY (*out of sight*): Yes!

SIMP: But I can't see! The wall's in the way.

FRANNY (*on box*): I'll stand here and tell you what he's doing.

FRANNY *gets on the box and looks over the wall.*

FRANNY (*over shoulder to* SIMP): Two balls in your left hand and one ball in your right. Left to the right and left to the right. Right to the left and right to the left. Left to the right and right to the left. Right to the left and left to the right.

SIMP *in total confusion. Balls dropping. Near to tears.*
BLUEY *appears over the wall.*

BLUEY: Got it?

SIMP (*unconvincingly*): Yes.

They wait for the display.
SIMP *throws all three balls up in the air together. They all fall.*
General gloom.

SIMP: This is hopeless. I know! Let's try the dancing first.

BLUEY: Yes. Dancing!

BLUEY *disappears and* SIMP *stands on the box. She watches as* FRANNY *goes through her dance steps.*

SIMP (*to* BLUEY *over the wall*): Left to the right and left to the right. Right to the left and right to the left. Left to the right and right to the left. Right to the left and left to the right.

There is a crash behind the wall.
SIMP *looks over the wall.*

SIMP: Oh heck!

BLUEY, *top hat askew and looking pained, looks over the wall.*

BLUEY: Oh no! I'll never learn to dance.

SIMP: I'll never learn to juggle.

BLUEY: What shall we do?

FRANNY: What shall we do?

SIMP: What shall we do? Hmmmm.

SIMP *walks about wondering what to do.*

FRANNY: I know. (*Pause.*) No. No.

BLUEY: Maybe . . . (*Pause.*) No. No.

Pause and then SIMP *has an idea.*

BOTH: What?

SIMP (*silently mouthing*): I know what we could do.

BOTH (*silently mouthing*): What?

SIMP (*silently mouthing*): We could take down the wall.

BOTH (*silently mouthing*): Take down the wall?

FRANNY (*shouting*): Take down the wall?

BLUEY: We can't!

FRANNY: We'll get into trouble.

BLUEY: It's not allowed.

SIMP: Only for a minute.

BLUEY: We can't.

FRANNY: We can't.

SIMP (*to* BLUEY): Just until you can dance.

BLUEY: Just until you can juggle?

FRANNY: No.

BLUEY/SIMP: Shhhhhh.

SIMP: Franny go and see if there's anyone coming.

SIMP *gives* FRANNY *the box.* SIMP *and* BLUEY *start to take down the wall. Music accompaniment. They are watching out for* MR MAN.

First two bricks slowly and then the pace quickens. FRANNY *joins in after third brick.*

Now there is a hole large enough for BLUEY *to come through. Both* SIMP *and* FRANNY *step back. Very very tentatively* BLUEY *comes through the hole in the wall. Music continues.*

BLUEY *is on the red side. He looks at the audience.*

BLUEY (*doing gesture*): Hello.

BOTH (*doing gesture*): Hello.

BLUEY (*doing gesture to audience*): Hello.

Encouraging audience to do it back to him.

SIMP/BLUEY: Juggling!

FRANNY: Shhh. I'll keep watch.

BLUEY: Right. Watch me!

He goes into a juggling routine. Very accomplished. Then slows it down.

Now together. One. Two. Three.

SIMP: One. (*Throws ball.*) Two. (*Throws ball.*)

BLUEY: Again! One. Two. Three.

SIMP: One. (*Throws ball.*) Two. (*Throws ball.*)

BLUEY: And again. One. Two. *Three.*

SIMP *tries again. And this time all three balls go slowly into the air in the correct manner.*

FRANNY: Yes!

SIMP *repeats a little quicker.*

SIMP: I can juggle. I can juggle!

FRANNY: Shhhh.

SIMP: Dancing!

This with a gesture to FRANNY. *They change places. Music.*

FRANNY: One, two, three, four.

BLUEY *is copying her steps behind her.*

BLUEY: One, two, three, four. One, two, three, four. One, two, three, four. One, two, three, four.

BLUEY, *with his eyes on* FRANNY, *gets better and better with each set of steps. He then dances without saying the numbers. He is very pleased.*

BLUEY: I can dance!

SIMP/FRAN: Hurrah!

FRANNY: Now try this.

Into a current dance step. BLUEY *likes it.* SIMP *joins in. Into a very noisy dance. All cheer. Then the rattle sounds offstage. They stop in horror.*

MR MAN (*off*): Franny! Simp!

Repeat rattle.

SIMP: The Man!

FRANNY: Bluey!

SIMP: The wall!

FRAN/SIMP: Hide!

FRANNY grabs a brick.
BLUEY gets on hands and knees.
The two of them sit on him to hide
him.
Enter MR MAN rattling his rattle.

MR MAN: Come on! Where are you?
What are you doing? This late and this
close to the wall? You're not supposed
to be here.

Turns his head round and back
towards SIMP and FRANNY.
BLUEY has moved round to keep out
of sight of MR MAN. SIMP and
FRANNY in sitting position move
round with him.

It's nearly dark and you're not meant
to be anywhere near this wall.

All three move again.

(*To* FRANNY) Do you know, if I
didn't know better, I'd say you were
holding a brick from the wall.

He turns. They move again.

And if I didn't know better I'd say
that . . . half the wall is gone. HALF
THE WALL IS GONE! What! What!
What! What! How did this happen???

FRANNY: It blew down.
SIMP: It fell down.

MR MAN: What?

SIMP: It blew down.
FRANNY: It fell down.

MR MAN: Which?

SIMP: The wind blew and it fell down.

MR MAN: Well we must rebuild it. Now.
Sooner. Instantly. Before the Blues
come through and eat us all. Rebuild
the wall. Rebuild the wall. Rebuild the
wall. Rebuild the wall!

He becomes frantic and faints.

FRANNY, BLUEY and SIMP look
at each other.

SIMP: Mister?

MR MAN (*half waking*): What?

SIMP: We must rebuild the wall.

MR MAN: Rebuild the wall.

SIMP: We'll do it if you go away.

MR MAN: Go away? Me? What?

SIMP: I mean keep watch. In case anyone
comes.

MR MAN: In case anyone comes. Yes.
The disgrace. Yes.

SIMP: Over here.

MR MAN: Over there?

SIMP: Go!

MR MAN (*going. Distraught and*
rattling): Rebuild the wall. Rebuild
the wall.

MR MAN exits.

FRANNY: Come on!

FRANNY shoves BLUEY back
through the wall.
Music begins.
We see BLUEY's sad face disappear.
They frantically rebuild the wall. They
pant.
FRANNY sees the blue balls. She
picks them up and hands them to
SIMP. She pockets them.

SIMP: We never said goodbye.

FRANNY: No. (*Calling.*) Hey Mister.
It's built.

MR MAN re-enters.
He looks at the wall. Palpable relief.
He wipes his forehead.

MR MAN: Ohhhh. That was a terrible
shock. You're lucky I'm still alive.
You young people have got no idea
what the Blues are like. If ever they
broke through that wall . . . Well it's
alright now. Everything back the way
it was, the way it should be. Now
come on. Home! (*He rattles.*)
Carnival tomorrow. Need to get some
sleep. Remember? Dancing?

FRANNY: Yes.

MR MAN: Yes. Dancing. Plenty of it.
But no juggling. Eh? Not from Simp
anyway, eh? Not in a million years.
Call yourself a juggler? Ha ha ha.

MR MAN *winks at* FRANNY.
FRANNY *smiles. She winks at*
SIMP.

MR MAN (*going*): Come on.

BOTH: Coming.

MR MAN *goes.*

SIMP: Call myself a juggler.

Music.
She has the blue balls. She juggles a
good display.
They both walk slowly from the wall.
A small noise and they turn back.

Slowly a brick is moving and then is
removed on the blue side.

A blue hand is seen. It places a blue
handkerchief in the space that has
been made.

SIMP *comes back to the wall and takes*
the handkerchief. She looks at it and
wraps it round her. She takes off her
red handkerchief and lays it in the
hole. She comes back to FRANNY.

The blue hand reappears and takes the
red handkerchief.

Pause.

The last brick is replaced.

Music continues.

And that is the end of our story. For
the first time since that fight at the
narrow bridge so many years ago a
Blue met with a Red and made friends.
What happens now, we don't know.
Because this happened just today.
Maybe you can tell how the story
will go on? For now, thank you, and
goodbye.

UNDER EXPOSURE

Written by Lisa Evans

For Juniors 9-13 Years Old

Under Exposure was first produced by the Women's Company of Theatre Centre on 9 March 1984, with the following cast:

NOMPI *a sixteen-year-old black South African girl*	Dorothy Brown
SUSIE *a young white English sports photographer*	Sally Eldridge
REJOICE *Nompi's mother*	Diane-Louise Jordon
THOKO *Nompi's cousin — who is in her early 20s*	Joan Williams

Written by Lisa Evans
Directed by Nona Sheppard
Designed by Helen Turner

Interwoven throughout the play are slides showing the reality of S. Africa and the singing of freedom songs.

Company together enter singing.

ONE (not NOMPI) SPEAKS: This is the story of Susie and the last dawn raid.

NOMPI: This is the story of Nompi, Susie and the last dawn raid. I'm Nompi. It was in the winter, I remember because I'd just had my sixteenth birthday and had to go to the government office for my pass book. I am dancing outside the football stadium to get some money for a ticket to the big match. I am not telling my mother where I am. If she knew I will be in big troubles. But she won't find out — she is at home.

REJOICE *is untangling the basket* NOMPI *has botched.*

REJOICE: Oh Nompukazi, what a mess you have made of this. I try to teach this daughter of mine how to make the baskets but all she is thinking of is football. I say to her 'you listen to your Mama Rejoice, that's me, we have to eat, your father Elias does not earn much at the factory, you are too old to play boys' games.' Ah, children! Today she took seven baskets to the market. I can see my Nompi now, getting a good price for them. She is a good daughter . . . most of the time.

NOMPI: Soon you will be meeting my cousin Thoko. She is on her way to Cape Town from the Ciskei — many many miles away.

THOKO: Can you see the bus yet? A cloud of red dust is all you will see at first, bumping along the dirt road to the camp. Then I will be on it and in three days I shall see Steve for the first time in eight months. He's my husband. We met at the university. He has to live in Cape Town now, for work. I will go to the men's hostel where he stays and shout: 'Steve, it's Thoko! I am here!' Have I got my pass book? Yes. Seventy-two hours, that's all I'm allowed to stay in Cape Town. But at least Steve and I will be together. Oh come on bus — come on!

NOMPI: Susie was a famous English sports photographer who came here to South Africa to take pictures of the big soccer match. She was staying at the Grand Hotel.

SUSIE *is on the phone. Pictures of 'White S. Africa' appear on screen.*

SUSIE: Hello. Susie Shelley, long distance. Sports desk please. Richard, hello. Just checked in — after thirteen hours of duty free! You'll get your soccer shots, you bet, lots of action . . . yes. Anyone'd think *The Herald* was paying for all this, not the South African Government! Oh, it's fantastic. I've taken a whole reel of film already — and that's just from my hotel window! Table Mountain, that's right. Must go, I'm off down to the sports stadium — I want to get some shots of local colour before the press meeting at lunch. Bye.

As she has been speaking shots of Table Mountain etc. appear on the screen.

NOMPI (*to audience*): The first time we met was a week before the big soccer game. I was dancing outside the stadium to earn some money for a ticket.

NOMPI *dances.*

SUSIE *enters, plus cameras, eating an orange.*

Look at the footwork ladies and gentlemens. This girl is going to be one fine footballer one day. Put your money in my tin and let me see the big match. Three cheers for the Kaizer Chiefs!

SUSIE *throws away the half-eaten orange. NOMPI watches where it rolls and darts to pick it up. SUSIE sees this and takes a photo. It comes up on the screen.*

NOMPI (*defensively*): Football players need vitamins.

SUSIE: Of course. Here. (*She holds out another orange.*) Go on.

NOMPI: I am not a beggar.

SUSIE: For the photograph.

NOMPI: O.K. (*She takes the orange nonchalantly but eats hungrily.*) Would you like to take my photo again.

SUSIE: O.K.

NOMPI *poses under the Cape Town football stadium sign.*

NOMPI: What are you doing please?

SUSIE: It's to do with the exposure. If you over expose a shot you let in too much light and if you under expose it, it's too dark and you can't see the image properly.

NOMPI (*who hasn't a clue*): Ah yes. Do you like taking photos?

SUSIE: Yes, I'm here to photograph the big match next week.

NOMPI: Really!

SUSIE: Yeah. It's my job, my newspaper in London sent me.

NOMPI: From London, England? (SUSIE *nods.*) Are you perhaps from London, Tottenham?

SUSIE: No but not far away.

NOMPI: You come all the way to South Africa when you could be paid to watch Tottenham Hotspurs in London!

SUSIE: Are you a Spurs fan?

NOMPI: Bowen, Hughton, O'Reilly, Perryman, Thomas, Archibald, Falco, Hoddle, Brazil, Crooks, Ardilles and Ray Clemence.

SUSIE: That's great! They won yesterday, 2 − 0.

NOMPI: I'm sure Clemence was good. Spectacular saves, like this. Into the corner, and push . . . away!

She demonstrates a flying save.

SUSIE: Not bad.

NOMPI: A corner. The mouth is dry, come on, mark him, you're blocking me, I can't see! Cross. A header and Nompukazi Tamana has made another brilliant save!

SUSIE: What are you like with a ball?

NOMPI: Terrific.

SUSIE: I met him once you know.

NOMPI: Who?

SUSIE: Ray Clemence. I was right on the touchline.

NOMPI: How near?

SUSIE: About like this.

NOMPI: You were that close to Ray Clemence?

SUSIE: I went up to him when the final whistle blew, shook his hand.

NOMPI: Did you!

SUSIE: Yes. Like this.

SUSIE *puts out her hand.* NOMPI *backs off reluctant.*

What's the matter?

NOMPI: I am not allowed. Trouble.

SUSIE: But I'm not South African. I'm English.

She puts out her hand again. NOMPI *takes it. Shakes.*

NOMPI: You touched me. You touched Ray Clemence. I shall never wash my hand again.

SUSIE: He was wearing gloves of course. And I have had the odd bath or two since then.

NOMPI: Thank you madam.

SUSIE: My name's Susie.

NOMPI (*to audience*): And that was how we met − Susie and me.

NOMPI *dances again.*

NOMPI: Miss Susie, Tottenham Hotspurs, they have black players don't they?

SUSIE: Yes, Garth Crooks. He was on loan at the beginning of the season, to

Manchester United, but it didn't work out.

NOMPI: Oh. Where is Manchester United?

SUSIE: In the north of England.

NOMPI: Is that far away?

SUSIE: About 200 miles.

NOMPI: And he is allowed to go there?

SUSIE: Yes, if he wants to. Why do you ask?

NOMPI (*to audience*): She didn't understand that here in South Africa, if you are black or coloured, you have to have a special stamp in your passbook to travel, especially into a white area — and that's where all the stadiums are. The last time I had my photo taken was at the Government offices. It was my sixteenth birthday and I had to apply for my passbook. The police official was white of course, with a face like a bullet and a voice to match.

NOMPI *plays* the POLICEMAN *too during the following.*

POLICEMAN: Hey you girl, face front you stupid kaffir. Can't you understand English?

NOMPI *poses for head shots which appear on screen.*

Hand.

She puts out her hand in handshake.

NOMPI (*to audience*): So I put out my hand.

POLICEMAN: For fingerprints girl.

NOMPI *turns over her hand.*

Name.

NOMPI: Nompukazi Tamana.

POLICEMAN: Are both your parents black?

NOMPI: Yes baas.

POLICEMAN: I don't think you are telling the truth. Your nose is too straight. There's some mixed blood

there somewhere. You know what it means if you are coloured?

NOMPI (*to audience*): I knew what he meant all right. It meant if he classified me as coloured I would be sent away from my family and made to live in another area, but he wouldn't listen to me. He said I was a stupid black. I told him I spoke three languages — English, Xhosa and Afrikaans — and that I'd only been at school for six years because I got ill with tuberculosis.

POLICEMAN: Excuses all the time you people. You know I am thinking your hair is not curly enough to be a black. Put this pencil in your hair and lean forward.

NOMPI *does so. The pencil stays in.*

OK. Now, you carry this passbook at all times, you hear? It states where you are allowed to live, play and work.

NOMPI: Yes baas, thank you very much baas.

She feels in her pockets for the passbook to show SUSIE.

NOMPI: It's not here! I had it in my pocket!

SUSIE: What's that?

NOMPI: My passbook — I must find it!

SUSIE: It's all right. Let me help you look.

NOMPI: You don't understand! I have to have it. If I am stopped they will demand to see it.

SUSIE: But if you explain.

NOMPI: I am in a white area without a pass, don't you see? I could go to prison for that!

SUSIE: Now calm down. Let's go through your pockets.

SUSIE *starts to search* NOMPI's *pockets.* NOMPI *instinctively freezes and raises her arms to be searched.* SUSIE *discovers the passbook in the top pocket and reads it.*

'Nompukazi Tamana. Classified as black.'

She notices NOMPI's *stance.*

What's the matter? Look I wasn't going to hurt you. I'm just here to take photos. If you like, I'll send you a copy of the one of you — okay?

NOMPI: Really?

SUSIE: Sure. What's your name, Nompu . . .

NOMPI: Nompukazi Tamana but everyone calls me Nompi.

SUSIE: Susie Shelley. And your address?

NOMPI: If you are sending it care of Mama Luke's store, Crossroads, it will be okay.

SUSIE: We have a TV series at home called Crossroads. It's a motel.

NOMPI: We have no motels in our Crossroads. Some people do live in cars though.

SUSIE: Really? Why don't I deliver the photo myself? I've got a couple of days free.

NOMPI: No. It is better not.

SUSIE: Why?

NOMPI: You won't get in.

SUSIE: Yes I will. Then you could frame it and put it up in your front room.

SUSIE *exits.*

NOMPI (*to audience*): Then I went home.

REJOICE *enters.*

It is a good house. That's my mother. She is called Rejoice. She is very proud of the house that my father built for us.

NOMPI *kicks her football around* REJOICE.

NOMPI: Mama, which is the front room?

The ball comes too close to REJOICE.

REJOICE: Take that football away now!

NOMPI *exits kicking the ball.*

REJOICE *shakes her head and continues making her grass baskets.*

SUSIE *enters taking shots of the squatter camp which appear on the screen.* REJOICE *watches her warily.* SUSIE *focuses to take a shot of* REJOICE.

REJOICE: Excuse me madam. Do you have permission to be doing that?

SUSIE: I'm sorry. Whose permission do I need?

REJOICE: Mine. It was my photograph you just were taking, wasn't it?

SUSIE: Well yes — and of Crossroads.

REJOICE: What for are you taking these photos?

SUSIE: I'm sorry. Do you mind?

REJOICE: My face is dirty and my hair is going in four directions at once. I don't want you to take away a picture of Rejoice as one messy woman. Wait a while.

REJOICE *washes her face in a tin bowl, smoothes her hair.* SUSIE *examines the baskets.*

SUSIE: Did you make these?

REJOICE: Well the grass does not grow that way. (*She laughs.*)

SUSIE: They're traditional designs aren't they? They're beautifully done. Are they for sale?

REJOICE (*laughing*): They are not very good to eat.

SUSIE: What tools do you use to make them?

REJOICE (*showing her hands*): These. I'll show you.

SUSIE: My mum tried to teach me to knit once. A scarf. It was so full of holes she unpicked it and reknitted it for me.

REJOICE: You buy some for your Mama, and for your sisters. They will like them.

SUSIE: There's only Mum to buy for.

REJOICE: Oh no. Why is that?

SUSIE: I'm an only child.

REJOICE: Only one? Your mother must be very sad. You take several for her. Poor woman. I had four children. Only one boy though.

SUSIE: I bet you spoil him rotten.

REJOICE: No. He is dead.

SUSIE: Oh. I'm sorry.

REJOICE: Yes. Three children I lost in the Ciskei.

SUSIE: That's one of the homelands isn't it?

REJOICE: It is not my home. My home is here with my husband. I was married, here in Cape Town, in church. I have a photo.

REJOICE *gets her wedding photo.*

SUSIE: Have you lived here long?

REJOICE: Oh yes. For many years. It is a good house. My husband Elias he fixed it well.

SUSIE: But you don't own it do you?

REJOICE: My child, this is South Africa, we are not allowed.

SUSIE: How do you feel about that?

REJOICE: Feel? I am with my family, my husband. I am one lucky woman. And nobody is sending me away!

SUSIE: What do you mean?

REJOICE: I don't think their mamas taught them good. They have no respect.

SUSIE: Who, the Government?

REJOICE (*suspicious suddenly again*): Why are you asking so many questions?

SUSIE: Actually I'm looking for someone. They pointed me in this direction at the store, but I lost count of the huts — houses.

REJOICE: Who are you looking for?

SUSIE: Her name's Nompukazi Tamana.

REJOICE: What has this girl been up to?

SUSIE: Do you know her?

REJOICE (*shaking her head*): Is she in troubles?

SUSIE: Oh no. I took her photo. I had it framed, look.

REJOICE *takes the photo, delighted, then squints and reads 'Cape Town Football Stadium'. Her mood changes.*

REJOICE: Nompi! Nompukazi Tamana come here at once!

SUSIE: You do know her.

NOMPI *runs on. Sees* SUSIE.

NOMPI: Susie! Hello. Welcome.

NOMPI *formally presents her hand to be shaken.* SUSIE *does so.*

SUSIE: Hello Nompi.

NOMPI (*to* SUSIE): I haven't washed it yet.

REJOICE: Haven't what Nompukazi?

NOMPI: Nothing. Nothing. Mama, I've just heard . . .

REJOICE: This woman has brought you a present, my child.

NOMPI: But Mama . . .

REJOICE: Don't you want to see it?

NOMPI: My photo? Really?

SUSIE: That's right.

REJOICE: Oh no, I think there has been a mistake. This cannot be my daughter here.

NOMPI: Let me see.

SUSIE: It is her.

REJOICE: No no. It cannot be her. My Nompukazi Tamana was yesterday all day at the market. She tells me so.

NOMPI: I was.

REJOICE: This is very odd because the girl in this photo is standing before the football stadium.

SUSIE: Oh hell. I'm sorry, I didn't mean to . . .

NOMPI: I can explain Mama.

REJOICE: Nompukazi Tamana, one more lie from you . . .

NOMPI: But Mama.

REJOICE: Don't you Mama me! Talking with strangers.

NOMPI: But Susie helped me find my passb . . . I mean . . .

REJOICE: You lost your pass?

NOMPI: No, I just couldn't find it for a moment.

REJOICE: You think this is a joke? You think we have the money to pay the fine if you are stopped and asked for the pass? You think you can kick your way out of jail perhaps. 'Oh yes, it is Nompukazi Tamana, famous footballer, we will let her go of course.'

NOMPI: No Mama, I don't but . . .

REJOICE: Football! I have enough of this football Nompukazi Tamana, are you hearing me?

SUSIE *exits to take more photos.*

NOMPI (*to audience*): I was hearing her. She was very cross. I can always tell because when I'm good I'm Nompi — bad, it's Nompukazi and when it's about football, it's Nompukazi Tamana — that's very cross. I was trying to tell her that my cousin Thoko was in the city. This was big news! We hadn't seen her for ages.

THOKO *enters.*

NOMPI: Thoko! You're here!

THOKO: Auntie. Nompi. (*They hug and kiss.*)

REJOICE: Thokozile my child! Nompukazi why are you not telling me your cousin is here?

NOMPI: Mam, I tried to but . . .

REJOICE: Thoko you are too thin.

NOMPI: I still have the football. Look.

REJOICE: Nompukazi Tamana, enough!

NOMPI (*to audience*): Football you see.

THOKO: They've taken Steve to jail.

REJOICE: Why?

THOKO: They wouldn't let me see him.

NOMPI: At the hostel?

THOKO: I asked at the wire and they said he was taken by the police. Political they said. I went to the jail but they said I cannot see him, that he is awaiting trial. They demand my pass. I have only a few hours left before I shall be sent back to the Ciskei but still they will not let me see him. They tell me to write!

REJOICE: You stay here daliwam. You are family. You stay. It is arranged. We will take care of you.

SUSIE *enters.*

NOMPI: Thoko, this is Susie. She is a famous photographer of football players. She knows Ray Clemence. Steve likes football. He took me to see the Kaizer Chiefs once. Susie, would you take a photo of me now, saving a goal, for Steve? Would you?

SUSIE: O.K.

NOMPI: And Thoko can be in it too. Thoko kick the ball to me.

REJOICE: Nompi.

NOMPI: Thoko, please? Are you ready Susie?

SUSIE: Yes okay, I'm ready.

NOMPI: Come on Thoko, please.

THOKO *gets up, picks up the ball and kicks it hard at* SUSIE.

NOMPI: Thoko! What did you do that for? (*To* SUSIE.) Are you all right?

THOKO: Take away your camera!

SUSIE: Look, you asked me!

THOKO: Not me. This face is not for your files!

NOMPI: Thoko!

THOKO: You have taken my husband, is that not enough?

NOMPI: But Susie hasn't done anything, she's my friend.

THOKO: She's white.

NOMPI: She's English.

THOKO: Whites make the laws.

NOMPI: That's not fair.

THOKO: Is it fair that I am not allowed to live with my husband? Is it?

REJOICE: Thokozile my child . . .

SUSIE: No of course not, but it's not my fault. There's no reason to . . .

THOKO: Is it fair that our homes are to be raided tonight by your white police?

SUSIE: What?

REJOICE: Again!

NOMPI: How do you know?

THOKO: A black policeman told me.

SUSIE: A raid, here?

NOMPI: You must go, Susie. They will set up road blocks.

SUSIE: What are they raiding you for, passes?

NOMPI: They say this camp is not allowed to be here. Please go — it is not safe for you here.

SUSIE: Yes but what about you?

REJOICE: This is our home.

SUSIE: If there's anything I can do . . .

THOKO: They *have* a photographer in the jail.

SUSIE: No, I mean, should I stay? Would it help?

THOKO: You?

NOMPI (*to audience*): I knew Susie wanted to stay but what *could* she do? It would be dangerous for her.

SUSIE: Goodbye then. (*She exits.*)

REJOICE: Go for water Nompi.

NOMPI: But we already have . . .

REJOICE: Nompukazi.

NOMPI: Yes Mama. (*She puts the bucket on top of her head, exits.*)

REJOICE: Fetch the pan with the mealie meal Thoko. And the oranges and plates. We have to eat.

THOKO *fetches the things from the hut.* REJOICE *makes the fire in the old oil-drum stove.*

THOKO: A man Steve knew was in that jail last year, Mama Rejoice, a union man also. He was in a cell alone. He had one orange only to eat each day.

REJOICE: Then we are blessed. We have an orange *and* mealie meal.

REJOICE: Here Thoko, eat.

THOKO: They torture them in there!

REJOICE: We will find us a lawyer.

THOKO: How can we do that if we are sent back to the Ciskei? If they raid tonight, we will be rounded up like cattle . . .

REJOICE: Your food is ready. First we eat. Then we sleep so our hearts are strong to stand together when the police come.

THOKO: How can we stand against bulldozers and tear gas?

REJOICE: Together we are strong. Nompi, what is taking you so long?

NOMPI (*entering*): There were five women at the tap.

REJOICE: Pour some in that bowl.

NOMPI: Are you all right Thoko?

REJOICE: Wash your hands. Here Thoko, eat. Nompukazi, I mean *both* hands.

NOMPI: I have Mama. (*She hasn't.*)

THOKO: I am not hungry.

REJOICE: Children!

NOMPI: We are not children.

REJOICE: One will not wash, one will not eat! I don't care if you *have* been going to the university – you are learning nothing. You must continue each day and until you are learning not to give up, to me you are children still!

Exasperated she leaves. Pause.

THOKO: Wash your hands Nompukazi.

NOMPI: Eat your food Thokozile.

Silence.

O.K?

THOKO: O.K.

NOMPI (*to audience*): They came at dawn the next day. (THOKO *exits during this speech.*) White police with dogs and tear gas. Driving bulldozers that knocked our houses, our homes, to the ground. Mama was proud of the home my father had built from the rubbish heaps of the city but the bulldozers lifted it in the air and then flattened it like a man kicking over an ant hill. (*She kicks over the shelter. Photos of a raid appear on the screen. Sound of a raid.*) Mama and I were stopped by the police and put on a bus to the Ciskei hundreds of miles away.

Photos of the barren 'homeland' appear on the screen.

REJOICE *enters carrying a rolled-up mattress on her head and the pans.*

The bus drives away. It is silent. Empty.

NOMPI: Mama, is this our homeland?

REJOICE: Help me with this.

NOMPI: But there's nothing here. Just a row of tin lavatories, scorched cracked earth. A dead tree. What are we to eat?

REJOICE *gets out an orange.*

REJOICE: We will share this.

NOMPI: Mama?

REJOICE: Yes my child.

NOMPI: When will we see my father again?

REJOICE: I don't know Nompi. At Christmas perhaps if he can afford the fare. Come, wash your face and hands first. Then we eat.

NOMPI (*as narrator*): We stayed in the Ciskei two days. Then Mama Rejoice said . . .

REJOICE: This is not my homeland – where children starve. My home is with my husband. We are going back to Crossroads.

They exit.

SUSIE *enters taking photos. As she does so the shots of the razed camp appear on the screen. She carries a large multi-coloured golfing umbrella. She is listening to a small radio.*

RADIO: And winter is certainly here in Cape Town. But even the rain is not putting off supporters who are already gathering outside the stadium for tonight's big match. Also raring to go are some of Britain's foremost sports pressmen and women – guests of the Ministry for Sport.

Unseen by SUSIE, THOKO *enters carrying a large piece of heavy plastic sheeting.*

I spoke briefly this morning to one of them, photographer Susie Shelley, who said 'I wouldn't miss this match for the world.'

THOKO: More holiday snapshots?

SUSIE: Thoko! I never thought I'd find you – I mean it's just gone, flattened. A rubbish dump.

THOKO: Yes, that is what it is like.

SUSIE: There was nothing about this in the papers or on the radio.

THOKO: It has happened before, many times. We are 'illegal squatters' you see. It is not news. The news is football. The news is Susie Shelley.

SUSIE: But it's inhuman!

THOKO: It is the law.

SUSIE: Where is Nompi? Is she all right?

THOKO: They use tear gas in the raids. She has weak lungs. How do you think she is?

SUSIE: Where is she?

THOKO: The Government gave them a 'free trip' also. To the Ciskei.

SUSIE: Oh no.

THOKO: And the Government have sent Steve to Robben Island. Do you know what that is?

SUSIE: Yes. A prison.

THOKO: If you look across the bay in good weather you can see it from Cape Town, twenty miles out.

SUSIE: How long is his sentence?

THOKO: The charge is political. A long time.

SUSIE: You're getting wet. Here take this.

She proffers the umbrella.

THOKO: You will get wet.

SUSIE: I can dry off later.

THOKO: At your hotel.

SUSIE: Yes.

THOKO: Do you have a bathroom there?

SUSIE: Yes.

THOKO: All to yourself, with hot water?

SUSIE: Oh look, my paper sent me here. It's my job.

THOKO: No, you look. You look. The people who did this — you are their guest. The radio tells the world Susie Shelley approves. She is here.

SUSIE: Yes, Susie Shelley is here, taking photographs of football. (THOKO *takes the umbrella.*) Look, sport here has changed. Now you have blacks and whites in the same teams, playing together, sharing the same dressing-rooms. Things are changing.

THOKO: And where do these black players go after the match? After you have taken their pictures to show the world how 'equal' it is here now? To this — or a black township or the hungerlands. No white lives like this. This big match is a whitewash and you are part of it.

SUSIE: Let me help.

THOKO: How?

SUSIE: If I take this, and you hold that end there . . .

THOKO: You whites! Always telling us what to do! This is my home! Listen. (*Singing underneath* THOKO*'s speech.*) Once upon a time there was a beautiful rich land. On the earth grew oranges, lemons, corn. Under the earth were gold and diamonds. The people were brown as freshly turned earth. Happy, strong, proud. It was their land.

Then traders came to their country — English and Dutch — and their skins were so white that the brown-skinned people thought they were ghosts who would never die. These ghost people were greedy and wanted land and gold. So they sent the brown-skinned people under the earth to dig out the gold and they took away the land the Africans had lived on for hundreds of years. And they said 'Your skins are black. Your gods are not the same as ours, so you will live apart from us.' And they made a law which they called Apartheid. And they made them carry passbooks which said, 'By the colour of your skin, this is where you are allowed to be.'

And the women said *NO*, and travelled from far and wide to stand together to say they would not carry passbooks. And they were beaten with sticks by the white ghosts' army. And the white ghosts became afraid and sent the brown-skinned people to barren areas of the country where nothing grew and there was no work, no food. And they said 'Here you will stay, apart from us, and we will call these places your homelands. You no longer belong in South Africa.' But they allowed the brown-skinned men to come to the rich white areas to work for them.

Hidden away in the barren homelands the brown-skinned people began to die. And the women said, 'What of us, without husbands? What of our children, without fathers? Our children who are forced to learn in a foreign tongue.'

And the children said *NO*. And the white ghosts' army fired on them.

And others said *NO*. And they were beaten until the blood ran out of their shoes.

And still the women said *NO*. 'Our gods are wise. Our skins and those of our children are beautiful. We will not move. Now you have touched the women you have struck a rock. You have dislodged a boulder. You will be crushed.'

That is our story.

SUSIE: What can I say.

THOKO: There will always be the singing.

REJOICE: Across the darkness the freedom songs.

THOKO: Africa's voice.

Singing as NOMPI *and* REJOICE *enter plus the bedroll and pans on their way back from the Ciskei.*

NOMPI (*to audience*): When we left the Ciskei we hitched a lift part of the way. Then we walked but finally I could walk no further. We got on a bus.

They mime the bus.

REJOICE: Nompi, take your elbows out of my ribs.

NOMPI: Look Mama, at the lilies by the river, bright red like flames!

REJOICE: Oh these metal seats! They

pack oranges better than this. Nompi, sit still.

NOMPI: We're going home! What makes the earth so red Mama?

REJOICE: The blood and tears of our people.

NOMPI: That sounds like Thoko.

REJOICE: We have one voice my child.

NOMPI: Look, an elephant, over there beside the peppercorn tree! She's so thin.

REJOICE: It is the drought. Nompi please be sitting still.

NOMPI: Are we nearly there yet?

REJOICE: Not far.

NOMPI: Will it take long?

REJOICE: I don't know.

Pause.

NOMPI: Are we nearly there *now*?

REJOICE: No! Be quiet child.

NOMPI: Yes Mama.

Pause.

What's the time?

REJOICE: Nompukazi enough!

Pause.

Why are you so anxious about time suddenly?

NOMPI: No reason.

REJOICE: Nompi.

NOMPI: It's just that it's the big match tonight and I wanted to hear it on a radio.

REJOICE: And I thought . . . Football!

NOMPI (*to audience*): She called me Nompukazi Tamana all the way back to Crossroads.

RADIO: With just a few hours left to kick off, this year's Cup match promises to give the sixty thousand crowd already assembled a gem of a game.

THOKO *and* SUSIE *are building up*

the shelter again.

NOMPI *and* REJOICE *enter.*

NOMPI: Mama, listen . . . Thoko! Susie, you!

SUSIE: You came back.

REJOICE: Thoko my child.

THOKO: Welcome home.

REJOICE: What a mess. Only men could have done this. Three days travelling to come home to this.

THOKO: Sit down, under the umbrella, there.

REJOICE: Oh that is better.

NOMPI: Tonight you will be at the big match.

SUSIE: Yes. Then I fly back to England tomorrow morning.

NOMPI: To Tottenham Hotspurs. Try and pass me.

NOMPI *gives* SUSIE *the football.*

SUSIE: O.K.

She gets the ball past NOMPI.

NOMPI: Offside!

SUSIE: How could I be offside?

NOMPI: There must be two players between you and the goalie when it's kicked to you.

SUSIE: But there's only you and me playing?

NOMPI: Exactly. Offside!

SUSIE: I've got a surprise for you.

NOMPI: What is it?

SUSIE: Here. (*She hands* NOMPI *an envelope.*)

NOMPI (*opening it*): For the match?

SUSIE *nods.*

Tonight?

SUSIE: Yes. Don't you want to go?

NOMPI: A ticket! A ticket! Mama, Susie gave me a ticket. Can I go? Please?

Please say I can. I promise I'll wash, and help you and never be bad again. Can I? Can I?

REJOICE: I give in.

NOMPI: I can?

REJOICE: I am saying so aren't I?

NOMPI: You mean yes? Say yes Mama.

REJOICE: Are you deaf as well as crazy? Yes!

NOMPI: Susie, can we go now?

SUSIE: O.K. We don't want to be held up tonight. I was stopped on my way in here the other day.

REJOICE: Nompi, your hat.

THOKO: Who by? Police?

SUSIE: Yes and a white man in a grey suit.

Tension.

THOKO: What was this man's name?

SUSIE: He was Chief Commissioner — for Co-operation and Development.

THOKO: Yes but what was his name?

SUSIE (*reading from her notebook*): Tomo van Nierkerk.

Silence.

REJOICE: My child, when did you see this man at Crossroads?

SUSIE: The day before yesterday. What's the matter?

THOKO: Wherever Tomo van Nierkerk is seen, two days later there is a raid.

SUSIE: Then there's going to be another raid tonight!

REJOICE: Who are these people who plague us? Have they not children? Have they not mothers who loved them? My Lord, witness. I will not forget what they are doing to my people until I go to the grave. I will not forget even once!

NOMPI (*shocked*): Mama.

SUSIE: But there's nothing left to destroy.

THOKO: Only our spirits.

REJOICE: They try to stop us singing. These people think they can stop the rain falling.

NOMPI (*handing the ticket back to SUSIE*): I must stay here. Thank you.

SUSIE: Look, Nompi can still come with me can't she? I'll look after her and at least she'll be safe with me.

REJOICE: And after the match?

SUSIE: I'll take her back to my hotel. Oh no, of course, I can't.

REJOICE *starts to gather their things together to bury.*

NOMPI: Why don't you stay here?

SUSIE: What?

NOMPI: Witness. Take pictures of the dogs and the sticks, the tear gas.

SUSIE: I have to be at the match. I'd lose my job. I can't. I just can't.

NOMPI: But I have seen white women at the raids.

THOKO: South African women. It is different. They can vote.

NOMPI: Please stay.

SUSIE: Nompi, I have to be at the match.

NOMPI: I don't know.

REJOICE: They must be buried.

NOMPI: I forgot.

THOKO: You forget too much Nompukazi.

NOMPI: That's not fair. I have a good memory.

THOKO: For the names of white footballers.

NOMPI: I know black ones too — Mapoyane, Baliac . . .

THOKO: Men's names. Men's sport. You are a woman, Nompukazi. A black woman. You forget who you are.

REJOICE: Children, help me. This is no time for football.

THOKO: You belong here. Have pride.

NOMPI: I know that. I do.

REJOICE: Here, this must be buried also. (*The corrugated iron.*)

SUSIE: But we've only just put it up!

REJOICE: And now we must take it down and hide it.

NOMPI *and* THOKO *fold the plastic.*

SUSIE: No Nompi, shake the water out first. . . if you fold it like that . . .

NOMPI: I will fold it my own way.

SUSIE: But you're doing it wrong.

THOKO: It's her way. This is our fight. Our country. We have waited too long for freedom your way.

SUSIE: It's not my way! I'm from England!

THOKO: And are all men and women equal in England, whatever their colour?

SUSIE: No.

THOKO: When you are all equal, when there is no prejudice, then you show us and maybe, maybe we will listen.

REJOICE (*kindly*): Susie, I tell my children, I tell you, we are women. We must stand together. Enough?

SUSIE *smiles and nods.*

They all start to sing and pack up the things under the plastic.

NOMPI (*to audience*): And so we buried all we owned and waited. I remember noticing that the tablecloth was over the mountain — a white cloud that meant Spring was coming. The light faded.

NOMPI: Thoko?

THOKO: Yes.

NOMPI: Will you stay beside me?

THOKO: Of course.

Pause.

Mama Rejoice, they won't let Steve out of Robben Island, will they?

REJOICE: No my child.

NOMPI: What are you going to do Thoko?

THOKO: Unga buzi.
[It is better you don't know.]

NOMPI: But why can't we know?

THOKO: Uku hamba kwam, amapolisa a za ku ni buza.
[When I am gone, across the border, the police will question you. I don't want you to be arrested too.]

NOMPI: U yoba i freedom fighter?
[You are going to be a freedom fighter?]

REJOICE: Nompukazi, u thetha kakhulu. Iza.
[Will you learn to hold your tongue. Come along.]

NOMPI (*to audience*): We talked in our own language so Susie could not understand. It was dangerous for Thoko. She was going across the border to become a freedom fighter.

SUSIE (*handing* NOMPI *the radio*): Here, keep this. At least you can listen to the match. Goodbye Nompi.

SUSIE *exits.*

NOMPI (*to audience*): So she left and I did not see her — my friend with the cameras — again. As dawn came the women began to sing — standing together, arms raised. Quietly at first but as the first bulldozers roared into Crossroads the voices grew.

As NOMPI *narrates we hear the sound of the raid, the singing, ululation. The three women are driven back and forth. Photos of the raid appear on the screen.*

The dogs were straining at their collars, teeth bared, reddened eyes bulging. Tear gas filled the air as the police drove us apart with their sticks, shouting and cursing. The dogs tore our clothes. Noise and more noise. Crashing of huts falling, the engines, men's voices driving us like wild cattle.

I began to run, blindly, the gas was choking me, burning my eyes and lungs like acid, raw red. I must find air. I lost Mama and Thoko. I couldn't breathe, I couldn't find them. I ran.

NOMPI *runs off. We hear* THOKO *and* REJOICE *calling her name. Onto the screen comes a picture of* NOMPI *limp in* REJOICE's *arms. Silence.* THOKO *leaves* REJOICE *alone on stage. We hear* REJOICE's *voice start to sing the* ANC *national anthem.* THOKO *and* NOMPI *join in. Sound of a jet taking off overhead. The women watch it. The singing continues.*

Voice Over AIR HOSTESS: *Good morning ladies and gentlemen. On behalf of Captain Shepphard and his crew I would like to welcome you aboard flight BA 724 to London Heathrow. The cabin crew will shortly be bringing round headsets for which we are obliged to make a charge of £2 or three Rand. The in-flight movie we are showing today is 'Trading Places'. We would ask you to remain in your seats until drinks have been dispensed. Luncheon will be served approximately two hours after take off. We hope you have enjoyed your stay in South Africa and that you will fly British Airways again.*

REJOICE, NOMPI, THOKO *and* SUSIE *continue to sing the anthem.* REJOICE *smiles for* SUSIE *to come closer to them. However the balance is the three black women together and* SUSIE *slightly apart. The last word we hear, as the three women raise their fists, thumbs raised, in the salute, is 'AFRICA!'*

THE SCHOOL ON THE GREEN

Devised by Greenwich Young Peoples Theatre

A full-day participatory programme
For Juniors 8-11 Years Old

The School on the Green is a full day participatory Theatre in Education (TIE) programme for third and fourth year pupils in primary schools which was first presented in the Spring term of 1984. The programme was re-worked and partially re-written for a second run in the Autumn term of 1985. It is this second version that is reproduced here.

The original version of *The School on the Green* was devised by a team of four actor/teachers, a director and a writer, the latter working with his ideas as they emerged during the process as well as initiating through his writing. By the time of the re-work, the writer, Chris Johnston, had left the company and changes and developments to the script were made by the company's new resident writer, John Wood. The final product is therefore the working fusion of the skills of two writers, two directors and six actor/teachers. The design was developed through the devising process in conjunction with the specialist skills of a designer. The set for this touring programme was based on four large double screens within which the action occurred, the use of realistic stage properties being an important feature of the set.

The programme deals with the topic of education, obviously the most immediate common experience of all children and therefore simultaneously very important and extremely difficult to tackle because of that. The overall objective is to help the pupils to develop their individual and collective potential for contributing to the processes of social change. This in turn entails the need to explore and understand the related concepts of autonomy, individualism, collectivity and cooperation, power, knowledge, conflict and change itself.

The vehicle chosen to facilitate this learning is the true story of the 1914 Burston School rebellion. The story is particularly potent because at its centre are the perceptions and actions of a group of young school children. The specific, concrete details of this story are used to engage the pupils with the following four questions which arise from the story but are also of immediate contemporary relevance. The central concepts of the programme are embedded in these questions:
1   Why does social conflict occur?
2   How do people change things?
3   What role should education have in a changing society and whose interests should it serve?
4   What do we mean by knowledge?
These questions provide the educational focus for the programme although they are never posed explicitly in this form. The pupils encounter them in different guises as they investigate the events of the Burston story.

The School on the Green is a fusion of presentational and participatory theatre. Thus, while the scripted scenes are reproduced fully in the following text, the participation sessions cannot be reproduced in the same way nor can the vital discussion sessions. These sections of the programme depend on the skills of the actor/ teachers involved and more fundamentally on a clear understanding of the learning areas contained within them.

We have therefore recorded here the underlying educational aims of such moments and the form in which they were contained rather than a verbatim account of the individual style of any one actor/teacher.

The programme was devised for four actor/teachers, all of whom played more than one role and shared the important function of co-ordinator. The co-ordinator is a combination of teacher and organiser, a function designed to enable and facilitate both the learning of the pupils and the mechanics of the programme. The co-ordinator introduces and stops each scene and runs any discussions with the whole group while the remaining three actor/teachers prepare for the next part of the programme.

An important aspect of the programme, which by its very nature cannot be recorded, is flexibility. *The School on the Green* is designed to be flexible and responsive to the needs of the pupils and the demands of time. Any company working on the programme needs to be aware of this fact, and the possibilities and potential offered to a group of skilled actor/teachers once the programme is in performance. Some of these possibilities are noted in the script but the limitations of space prevent an exhaustive list of these being included.

It is useful to note that two other TIE companies used the original script before it was re-worked. Both were successful in using the core of the programme and its aims while developing its potential to suit their own artistic and educational needs and those of their audience.

Finally, Greenwich Young Peoples Theatre works in close liaison with the teachers whose classes we visit. Preparation and follow-up work are considered vital and are presented in a pack to accompany the programme. Copies can be obtained from the company on request. However, since the preparatory work for *The School on the Green* was effectively the start of the programme, some reference must be made to it here.

Each school was given a video made by the company which introduced a member of the team and the character she was to play in the programme. Using the pictures of rural life that were reproduced on four screens (the basis for the set) Dossy, an elderly Norfolk woman, introduced the pupils to the background of rural England in 1914, this information being central to their participation in the programme. The video was accompanied by a transcript and notes for the teacher to use with their class. The actor/teacher used in the video then became the initial contact person for the pupils when the team went into schools and it is Dossy's story around which the programme is constructed.

Lynne Suffolk,
Greenwich Young Peoples Theatre, 1987

The School on the Green was first produced by the Greenwich Young Peoples Theatre in the Spring of 1984, with the following cast (over two runs):

ACTOR/TEACHERS	Roger Chamberlain, Yasmin Sidhwa, Viv Harris, Euton Daley, Anne Woolford, Rob Tiplady
MUSICIAN	Robbie McGovan
PROGRAMME DIRECTORS	Chris Vine, Lynne Suffolk

Written by Chris Johnston
Additional material by John Wood
Designed by John Daniell

Set painting by Neil Appelt
Costumes by Fay Barratt

Teacher's Notes devised by Euton Daley
Teacher's Notes edited by Sue Bennion

Greenwich Young Peoples Theatre is funded by the Inner London Education Authority, the Arts Council of Great Britain and the London Borough of Greenwich.

Introduction in the Classroom: The programme starts with the four actor/teachers meeting the pupils in their own space — their classroom. In order to break down the formality of the classroom situation, teachers are asked to organise the pupils in a semi-circle of chairs. The aims of this preliminary session are:
1   To make contact and an initial 'contract' with the pupils.
2   To enable the team to 'read' and get to know the pupils and vice versa.
3   To introduce the topics of education and collective action in a present-day context.
4   To encourage the pupils to talk, to express their own opinions in an informal atmosphere.

The Form: The actor/teacher playing Dossy talked to the group about the video, introduced the company and explained briefly what the day would be about and the sort of work that would be done.
   A valuable device during this introductory session was the use of frozen pictures created by the actor/teachers to represent particular attitudes that pupils have towards school. This was used to introduce the pupils to a technique which is employed throughout the programme, that of 'tableaux' or 'depiction'. These carefully constructed pictures capture a wealth of precise meanings and, like the freeze frame on a video, can be studied at leisure. Thus the pupils were invited to 'read' these first, quite simple, pictures and were then divided into three groups, each with an actor/ teacher, to discuss their ideas about school. In order to ensure mixed-ability grouping the teacher was asked to select the groupings before our arrival and a colour identification was used for each group. Areas of questioning included:

What is education for?
Why bother to go to school?
Who says you have to go?
Where does education/learning take place?
Have you ever taught anyone?
Who decides what you should learn in school?
Are there some things those people would say should not be taught in school?
Do you think there are things you should not learn about?
If there was something happening at school that you thought was wrong is there anything you could do to change it?
The group discussions lasted for ten minutes. The pupils were then taken to the hall.

Introduction in the Hall — Underlying Aims:
1   To enable the pupils to share their excitement with each other and the team in an informal way.
2   To help the pupils to begin to make the set (i.e. the space they would be working in all day) their own.
3   To enable the actor/teachers to check how much of the background to the period had been assimilated.

Form: The pupils were encouraged to explore the set and look at and talk about the large pictures which they had already seen on the video.
   The pupils were then called together onto the 'Green' (a green circle of carpet) and, in a style already established on the video, an actor/teacher 'became' Dossy, by putting on the Dossy costume and going into character in front of their eyes.
   During the following script the pupils remained seated on the 'Green'; the action took place all around them.

The Burston Story Introduction

DOSSY: Hello there, 'as a funny thing me coming to talk to you. I haven't bin in a school since I was a girl an thas a long time ago. When I was at school we had a slate like this and wrote words we copied offa the blackboard.

DOSSY *and* ACTOR/TEACHERS *get out their slates and write their names.*

Thas a long time ago — thas when I was called Dossy afore I got married. Thas a long time ago — seventy years. But I still remember it, I remember the songs we used to sing

A/Ts *start singing first verse of* 'England Arise'.

and the lessons we was taught.

DOSSY *joins in the song. It finishes. Congratulations among group which* DOSSY *cuts across.*

But I also remember the day at was all took away from us. When I heard I cried, I broke me little heart, but my sister Marjory she say 'Dossy stop crying, we're doing something about this.'

A/T: An you did.

A/T: An you won.

A/T: All of you together.

DOSSY: Thas seventy years ago now but that still makes me smile to think about it. How us kids said 'No'.

A/T: No.

A/T: No.

A/T: No.

ALL: No.

DOSSY: You can't take this away from us.
    As ours.
    Not yours.

ALL: An we ain't letting go of it.

DOSSY: That'll make you smile, that might make you feel sad as well as angry sometimes, but I'm going to tell you what it was we had, and then you can see if it was right that they should ha' tried to take that away from us.

Sound of scythe being sharpened. Continues . . .

I'm going to start over seventy years ago. I was born in a little village in Norfolk.

A/T: Morning farmer Fisher.

A/T: Morning Reverend. Mrs.

A/T: Morning.

DOSSY: Burston. That'd only got one shop —

Sound of shop bell.

Boultons — that sold everything.

A/T: Quarter of tea.

A/T: Quarter of tea.

A/T: Half of cheese.

A/T: That'll be sixpence.

A/T: Sixpence?

DOSSY: If you could afford to buy it. My mother and father worked on the farm, they were farm labourers and they worked for Mr Fisher. My mother were only employed on casual labour — that's not all the year round, just when there was a lotta work on like potato pulling and suchlike.

After a moment the scythe stops.

Them days I stayed with my granny.

A/T: Once upon a time in a land far far to the East . . . and they all lived happily ever after. Our Father which art in heaven.

A/T: Hallowed be thy name.

A/T: Thy kingdom come.

All continue with prayer — under DOSSY.

DOSSY: Thas my first memory sitting at home with her. The next is of going to church of a Sunday and that red-faced Reverend pointing his finger at us in church.

A/T: And you shall walk in the path of righteousness!

DOSSY: I cried. (*Sound of slap.*) I got a slap. I thought we'd done something wrong, but my mother said that were only his way o' making us better people.

Lord's Prayer finishes and swells to an 'Amen'.

Then I got old enough to lead the horses down to the field.

She stands and mimes. Horse sounds.

A/T: Careful now Dossy.

DOSSY: There weren't no tractors then it was all beautiful horses.

A/T: Don't let em run away with you.

DOSSY: Big as trains they were, huffing and steaming, pulling ploughs.

A/T: Oh Dossy.

A/T: Lead em on Dossy.

DOSSY: At was a real treat when I was old enough to lead them. (*She sits down.*) I was six years old. That was like heaven to me. 'Cos I din know no better at that age. Then I was told I was going to have to go to school.

ALL A/Ts: Once once is two; two twos is four, etc.

Establish and then keep under next.

DOSSY: School. I didn't want none o' that. Did I cry. I was a great one for crying. (*Sound of slap.*) Anyway I gotta good slap and told I gotta go, so I went. It weren't like this. Our school was one room an all the children from six to thirteen we had lessons together — eighty of us.

The two times table continues plus a sing-song alphabet.

Out with the slates and copy off the blackboard. Little-uns faced one way with a teacher and big-uns faced the other teacher and off we went at it. When they thought you was tall enough you moved across. I didn' think much to it, nor did the teachers we had, 'cos when I'd been there two weeks they up and left!

The 'lessons' end in a cheer.

So I thought, thas school, I've done with that, and I went back to helping with the horses and helping my sister Marjory picking stones up off the field.

Sound of scythe starts. DOSSY *begins to pick up stones and put them in a bucket.* A/T *endowed as* FARMER *walks round to* DOSSY.

FARMER A/T: Wages.

Six pennies are counted into her tin. THE FARMER *moves on to another* A/T *and holds out hand.*

FARMER A/T: Rent.

SECOND A/T *counts out all the pennies from a tin. It is not enough* — A/T *goes to* DOSSY *and holds out tin. She reluctantly drops her money into it.* SECOND A/T *gives it to* THE FARMER *who pockets it and leaves.*

DOSSY *shows the pupils her empty tin and starts picking stones again.*

DOSSY: But then we heard there was two more teachers coming. I cried. (*Sound of slap.*) I got slapped. At was my sister saw 'em. It was dark, she were looking out the bedroom window — nosy girl — always was.

DOSSY *brings the* A/Ts *together.*

She say 'Dossy come here.'

The window is established. A/Ts *peering out.*

'Look at them. Can you see?'

'Littlest' A/T *shakes head.*

'There's two of them. They got a big suitcase. He's tall.'

DOSSY: Well that's how she first saw them. A week later we were in school again (*Sound of slap.*) — me with red eyes. But that weren't like the same place. We sang songs, we sat out on sunny days, we went and watched the horses in the fields, we went down to the river, we had magic lantern shows in the dark, we talked about the stars, about the sun, about the seasons, I went around with me eyes wide open. My mum say

ALL A/Ts: Dossy I ain't ever seen you so happy.

A/Ts *break from their relationship close to* DOSSY.

Well, I never learnt so much as I did in them three years and that was all because of them two new teachers.

A/T: Mr and Mrs Higdon, Tom and Annie.

DOSSY: Them two loved us to learn. I'll never forget them. My mother afore she died remembered them. That whole village took to them and thas not something Norfolk people do — take to strangers right off, but they did with them, even that reverend.

A/T: On behalf of the managers, Farmer Fisher, Farmer Sterne, I'm delighted to congratulate Mr and Mrs Higdon on a very successful conclusion of their first school year. Our warmest thanks.

Clapping and polite talk.

DOSSY: But then something went wrong. We knew something was up, not just the war we all knew was coming — my uncle Ron was killed in the first week in the trenches in that war. But it weren't war talk that Marjory and me heard when she — nosy — used to listen at the bedroom door. That was talk about the Reverend and Farmers, and Mr and Mrs Higdon.

A/T: The *Higdons* care *nothing* for the *health* and *morals* of those children.

A/T: They been *filling* their *heads* with a lotta *nonsense* I've heard.

A/T: *Lies*, I never thought I'd hear a man of *God* speaking such blatant *lies.*

This is done as a round — confused sentences with the odd word standing out.

DOSSY: I didn't understand it. But I were having to listen through the door.

After a few beats the round finishes. Silence . . .

Today we're going to open the door so you can hear what they was talking about, so you can find out what happened the day my sister Marjory went to school and heard Mr and Mrs Higdon had been dismissed.

A/T: Dismissed.

A/T: Dismissed.

A/T: Dismissed.

DOSSY: Yes, dismissed. And instead of doing what I did — sit and cry — you see if you can understand why.

Two A/Ts exit whilst whispering a chorus of 'dismissed' whilst the A/T playing ANNIE HIGDON *endows herself with appropriate costume. She then crosses and sits in front of the 'school' screen.*

Mrs Higdon. Dismissed.

Whispers stop.
A/T *playing* REVD. ELAND *enters and delivers letter to* ANNIE HIGDON. *She reads it. He leaves.*

ANNIE H.: If you're looking through the window Reverend, I'm tearing it up. Look. See.

She hesitates and puts the letter away.

DOSSY: It was then my sister Marjory came in with a bunch of flowers. Here, I'll show you.

DOSSY *takes off costume, picks up flowers and enters the scene as* MARJORY BRANDON.

MARJORY: Good morning, Governess. What's going on? Are we going on another walk?

ANNIE H.: There'll be no classes today, Marjory.

MARJORY: Is there measles again?

ANNIE H.: No, Mr Higdon and myself have been dismissed.

MARJORY: Does that mean you won't be teaching us any more?

TOM *comes in, pushing a cart/wheelbarrow.*

TOM HIGDON: Well, at least we've got a cart.

ANNIE H.: Marjory, you can go and put these flowers into water.

MARJORY *starts to go but stops at the doorway.*

ANNIE H.: Goodness, wherever did it come from?

TOM H.: I met Barney down at the Mill. He hears we're going to stay there. And he's coming to give us a hand.

ANNIE H.: Well, at least we've got friends!

TOM.: The whole village is talking. And it's not just talk.

ANNIE H.: We've had a visitor.

She gives him the letter. He reads it.

He says the new teacher's coming and we've half an hour to clear the schoolroom.

TOM H.: Half an hour? They told us a day.

ANNIE H.: Well it's changed.

TOM H.: So the truth don't get out . . . Where is he?

ANNIE H.: No Tom, it won't do to make it a personal issue.

TOM H.: They don't want teachers, they want a dog that barks. Just when people are starting to listen, starting to move. Just when we're beginning to make progress — that's when the forces of reaction come down.

MARJORY: Mr Higdon, I picked these for you. You won't be leaving us will you?

TOM H.: The Managers say we're not good teachers. Do you agree?

She shakes her head.

ANNIE H.: Marjory, fetch my camera — and pack it up as I've told you. Tom, let's finish loading.

MARJORY: No, I won't. We need the camera for our lessons.

TOM H.: Don't be disrespectful to the Governess.

MARJORY: But why? I don't understand! Why do you have to go? . . .

The Co-ordinator then stops the action by saying 'Freeze'. The actors hold the picture whilst The Co-ordinator presents the following questions to the pupils:

CO-ORDINATOR: Two popular teachers being dismissed?
Pupils being rude to teachers?
Teachers being rude to School Managers?
What's going on?

The Co-ordinator then tells the actors to 'relax'. The picture is dissolved and the Co-ordinator leads a discussion with the pupils about what they have just seen. (This technique of freezing the action abruptly, holding the picture whilst a series of 'headline' questions are asked and then instructing the actors to relax before initiating a discussion with the pupils is used by the Co-ordinator throughout the investigation.)

Setting up the investigation — The discussion session which follows this first scene has a number of underlying aims:

1   To engage pupils with the 'problem' and introduce the central question.
2   To give them status.
3   To make a 'contract: between pupils and actor/teachers.
4   To explain the form of the investigation.
5   To empower them to make decisions.

The Form: The Co-ordinator encourages the children to speculate on why the two teachers were dismissed. Their ideas are recorded on a chart.

The notion of an investigation is introduced and a contract made, i.e., the pupils agree to carry out an investigation with the actor/teachers in order to try to discover some answers to our central question: 'Why were two popular teachers dismissed?' This question is hung on part of the set as a focus for the investigation. (A central divergent question is designed as a starting point through which to explore the learning areas. There is never one answer to a central question, for its aim is to open up further more complex questions for the pupils.)

The Co-ordinator then reveals six pictures showing incidents that happened to the teachers during the three years that led up to their dismissal. It is explained that they all happened at different times in the story and did not necessarily follow on from each other. However, each picture can be brought to life by the actors so the pupils can examine the 'evidence' for their investigation. Each picture is a frozen moment from the six scenes and each has a title underneath it.

1   Farmer Sterne Takes a Tumble.
2   Annie Makes a Fuss.
3   School Outing.
4   Late Night Lesson.
5   Grandad Goes to School.
6   Sharpening the Sickle.

It is explained that (1) and (2) involve the teachers and school managers; (3) and (4) involve teachers and pupils; and (5) and (6) involve teachers and parents.

The children are then asked to study the pictures and decide by talking to each other which event they would like brought to life first, i.e., we will be bringing all the events to life today but where do you think it would be best to start our investigation? Which pair of important events do you want to bring to life first? After taking some of their ideas and asking the reasons for their choice, the Co-ordinator organises a vote. Once a decision is reached the chosen pictures are moved to the top of the picture board. The pictures can be chosen singly with discussion after each event.

The Investigation: Each of the six pictures is brought to life in the form of presentational theatre, participatory theatre or a combination of the two. The script indicates which form each scene takes and whether it is fully scripted, improvised or a combination of the two.

The role of the Co-ordinator:

At the start of each scene the Co-ordinator:

1   discusses with the pupils what might be happening in the picture while the actors prepare set and costumes;
2   asks the actors to reproduce the picture;
3   names the characters in the picture;

4   describes the setting;
5   where necessary prepares the group for their participation: explaining the context, giving them any necessary information and forging a 'contract' with them;
6   winds back the action (like a video) to the picture at the start of the scene (in our version only the picture for 'Grandad Goes to School' was taken from the start of the scene);
7   gives the instruction — 'ACTION'.

After each scene the Co-ordinator:
1   freezes the scene, delivers the 'headlines', and then releases the actors;
2   sends the pupils to their 'home' groups to discuss what they have just experienced or prepares them for the next scene after the first of a 'pair' of events.

After each group session the Co-ordinator:
1   calls the pupils together again;
2   discusses with them which scene they wish to see next;
3   organises the vote.

The Co-ordinator for each scene changes according to the actor/teachers needed to perform in that scene.

Group Discussion: After each pair of scenes the pupils return to their 'home' groups. If possible they are given a few moments to talk amongst themselves before being joined by 'their' actor-teacher who draws out the clues they have discovered and discusses them.

Underlying Aims:
1   To unravel and/or develop the young people's understanding of what they have just seen.
2   To challenge and question the pupils' views and comments in order to reveal contradictions and address the overall aims of the programme through the Central Divergent Question: 'Why were two popular teachers dismissed?'

These sessions are vital to the programme and specific questions are suggested relating to each scene; however many of the questions will depend on the pupils' initial 'clues'. Each discussion should build on the last, enabling interconnections to be revealed and discussed.

The Scenes

1 Farmer Sterne Takes a Tumble

Characters: Marjory Brandon — Senior pupil
                Tom Higdon   — Assistant teacher
                Farmer Sterne — School Manager

Setting: Outside in one of Farmer Sterne's fields.

Form: Scripted presentational theatre. This scene uses the technique of freezing the action at four key moments. Like using the pause button on a video this enables the pupils to examine more carefully the rapid series of events which lead to a moment of violence.

FARMER S.: Right Marjory, same as usual. Three basket loads, then you can take a break. Filled right up to the top, mind, or you don't get your sixpence!

CO-ORDINATOR: Pause. (*The frozen picture is held for three beats.*) Action.

FARMER STERNE *moves away.* TOM HIGDON *enters.*

TOM H.: 'Ere Farmer Sterne, what's going on? Majory, it's well past nine o'clock.
Mr Sterne you know as well as I do that this is against the law.

FARMER S.: Stop meddling man!

CO-ORDINATOR: Pause . . . Action.

FARMER S. (*calling*): Marjory! (*She moves to his side.*)

TOM H.: She's not your property. (*He goes towards her* — FARMER STERNE *stops him.*)

CO-ORDINATOR: Pause . . . Action.

FARMER S. (*pushing* TOM *away*): Get back to the schoolroom where you belong.

TOM H. (*under his breath*): What! . . . You . . . No. (TOM *lunges at* STERNE *and pushes him over.*) Come along Marjory.

CO-ORDINATOR: Pause . . . Action.

MARJORY: You've hurt him!

FARMER S. (*propping himself up*): I'll get you Higdon!

CO-ORDINATOR: Freeze . . . (*The actors hold the picture.*)

Headlines: Farmers breaking the law?
School Managers keeping children away from school?
Teachers hitting School Managers?

CO-ORDINATOR: Relax actors. (*The picture is dissolved.*)
What have you discovered there to help our investigation?

The Co-ordinator then leads a discussion whilst the next scene is prepared, or sends the
pupils to their 'home' groups to discuss what they have seen.

Sample Questions
Why did Tom hit Farmer Sterne? If you were Tom how would you have dealt with the
situation? Who was breaking the law? Was Tom right to hit him? Why was Marjory
working in the field? Where should she have been? Why was a School Manager keeping
a child from school?

2 Annie Makes a Fuss

Characters:	Annie Higdon	— Headteacher
	Reverend Eland	School Managers
	Farmer Fisher	

| *Setting:* | In the schoolroom one afternoon when the children have gone home. |

| *Form:* | Scripted presentational theatre. |

FISHER: Are we interrupting?

ANNIE: I'm sorry, I was just preparing for tomorrow's class.

FISHER: We are interrupting.

ANNIE: The school is always open to its managers. Especially if they've come on matters of school improvements.

REVEREND: Is it a Daguerrotype, Mrs Higdon?

ANNIE: No, it's a dry plate field camera. Handsome, don't you think?

REVEREND: How does it serve in the children's education?

ANNIE: It demonstrates how photographs can be made. We'll be taking some pictures of the flowers we've collected.

REVEREND: Photography is not education.

FISHER: Our Mrs Higdon is one of these modern women. New kinds of teaching. They all want the vote nowadays. I'm dead against it. But if she can do the job then . . . Would you fetch the attendance register, please?

REVEREND: The disciples, Mrs Higdon, had no need of cameras.

ANNIE: Until I learn to perform miracles, Reverend, I'll use the proper equipment.

FISHER: The register.

ANNIE: I'm glad you called, gentlemen, since there are one or two matters I want to discuss concerning the children's health.

FISHER: Would you fetch the register or you'll try my patience!

REVEREND: So sorry to have inconvenienced you. (*She goes.*)

FISHER: Is she always so impertinent?

REVEREND: Did you know she's stopped coming to Church?

FISHER: Well, they do say she's a good teacher.

REVEREND: Yes, but if she doesn't come to Church . . .

FISHER: Sssh . . .

She comes back.

ANNIE: Here you are, gentlemen. I think you'll find it in good order.

FISHER: Let's hope so.

REVEREND: I'm sure we will.

ANNIE: May I discuss school matters?

REVEREND: Why has this boy Cotterrill been absent so often?

FISHER: Never mind Cotterrill, Reverend.

ANNIE: Mr Fisher will explain as how he's been working in the fields.

FISHER: Very important work.

ANNIE: The matter I wanted to raise concerns the roof.

FISHER: What's wrong with it?

ANNIE: It's leaking. You can see the hole up there where the rain comes in. That section of the schoolroom is completely unusable. And we're not receiving enough coal for the fires. The children get terribly cold. I've written on these matters but received no reply.

FISHER: The school has no money for further expenditure.

ANNIE: But the children are suffering.

REVEREND: Let the suffering children come unto the Lord — you, Mrs Higdon, must provide the warmth of His teaching.

ANNIE: I'd prefer a few sacks of coal.

FISHER: Thank you. (*Returning the register.*)

REVEREND: What's this? (*Indicating blackboard.*)

ANNIE: It's the words to a song we are learning.

FISHER: We are all, Mrs Higdon, servants to our masters.

ANNIE: Shouldn't we rather be servants to our children?

REVEREND: I'm concerned about the children's religious instruction.

Exits.

FISHER: More hymns, Mrs Higdon, more hymns.

Exits.

ANNIE: Good day to you gentlemen. I trust these matters will be raised at the next Managers' meeting?

CO-ORDINATOR: Freeze . . . and pause it there please . . . Can the School Managers come back . . . (*They do so and hold a position.*) . . .

Headlines: School Managers letting schoolchildren suffer?
Vicar telling teachers what to teach?
Teachers being very rude to visitors?

CO-ORDINATOR: What have you discovered there to help our investigation?'
Relax actors. (*They exit.*)

Sample Questions
What was Annie making a fuss about? Wasn't she a bit rude? Did she have to shout at them? Why? How would you have dealt with the situation? What did the Managers think of the way Annie taught? Surely photography is a waste of time? What was it that Farmer Fisher thought was more important than school work for Cotterrill?

3 School Outing

Characters: Annie Higdon   — Headteacher
Bet Phillips   — Pupil's parent and farmworker
Ben Philpotts   — Pupil
Reverend Eland — School Manager

Setting: In the schoolroom at the start of morning school.

Form: Combination of scripted theatre and participatory drama. The children are in role as the Burston school pupils throughout this scene. The Co-ordinator sets up the context and the drama starts when MRS HIGDON enters the classroom.

ANNIE HIGDON: Good morning, children. And what a lovely morning it is! Now let's see, who have we got missing? Ah yes, poor Sammy, he's obviously still unwell with the whooping cough . . . and – oh, no Ben I see. That's not like him to be late. We'll have to see what he has to say for himself when he arrives. Now then this morning we are concentrating on our mathematics. I was very pleased with your reading and writing, so now let's see if you can do as well with your mathematics! Remember yesterday at the end of school I asked you to see how many of Farmer Fisher's fifteen cows you could see in his fields on the way to school today? Well, how many did you count . . .? 12, good. Let's write that up on our blackboard. 12. So if each of Farmer Fisher's cows yields 4 pints of milk, how many pints will he have altogether? . . . Yes, 48 pints . . .

At around this point the A/T *playing* BEN *appears in the 'doorway'. He is clearly upset.*

ANNIE: Ah, so there you are Ben . . . what's kept you? . . . (*No reply.*) Come over here my dear. (*Beckons him.*) Well, what is it? What's a matter? . . . (BEN *is fighting back tears and whispers in* ANNIE's *ear . . . She comforts him.*) Go and sit down Ben. (*He does so.*)

ANNIE: Children, Ben has brought me some very serious news and I must share it with you, for it affects us all. As you know, Sammy Phillips has been away from school for quite some time now as he's been very ill with whooping cough. I'm sorry to have to tell you children that last night Sammy died. Now we're all going to feel very upset and miss Sam a great deal. We shouldn't be afraid of death, it is something that comes to us all but it is right to feel sad when we lose someone close to us. Usually when we feel sad we try to put out of our minds the thing that's making us sad . . . but if we do that now it means that Sammy's memory will die too and we must not let that happen. We can keep Sammy's memory alive by remembering and sharing the good, happy times we had together with him. Ben?

BEN: Yes, Mrs Higdon?

ANNIE: I know that you were a very good friend of Sam's. I wonder if you would share with the class a memory that you have of a time that you spent with him. A memory of a good, happy time. Would you do that dear?

BEN: Yes, Mrs Higdon. I used to play 'had' with him in the playground. Oh yes, I remember when we went to get some apples in Farmer Sterne's orchard and when Sammy was half-way up one of the trees, his trousers got caught on one of the branches and they ripped right up the backside!

ANNIE (*mock sternly*): And what did his mother say when he came home with ripped trousers?

BEN: She wasn't very pleased.

ANNIE: I imagine she wasn't very pleased . . . Did you get any apples? Would somebody else share a memory they have?

Draw out three or four children to share 'memories'. If they find it difficult 'remind' them, e.g. 'I know you used to play football with him – what position did he play?'

ANNIE: Thank you. We all have memories that we can share and so keep the memory of Sam alive. And if you notice one of your friends on their own in the schoolyard or perhaps walking home from school and they're looking sad and you think that it's thinking of Sam that's making them sad – go over to that friend and talk together about him and the good times.

Now, I expect the funeral will take place tomorrow and I very much want to go today to Sam's house to see his mother and to see his body which is waiting there until the time of the funeral, so that I can say goodbye. Children, I am going to ask you a question which I would like you to think very carefully about before you answer – Would anyone like to come with me? It will not be an easy thing to do, it will be very hard. And so you must decide for yourselves what to do, only you know what is the correct thing for you. So you must make up your minds whether to come or to stay here. Everybody who does come, I think, it would be good if you could think of one kind thing to say to Mrs Phillips. She has had a dreadful shock and is going through a very difficult time, so we must find any way that we can to help her. Perhaps those of you who decide to come could think of one kind thing to say to her when we get to her house. I shall take the flowers we've collected for the classroom. Now, can I see who's decided not to come?

Thank you, I know you've made the right decision for yourselves. I trust you to wait here until we return. Ben, please stand out front, all those who are going, please line up in twos behind Ben. When everyone is ready, please lead the way.

If necessary speak to the children who've decided to stay behind. MRS PHILLIPS *greets the children at her door – they all go behind the screen,* BEN *asks them to stand around the coffin.* ANNIE *comes in last.*

MRS PHILLIPS: Thank you for coming to say goodbye to my Sam. He'd have been pleased to know you cared so much. I'll just leave you alone with him for a few minutes.

She takes the cloth off the coffin and leaves.

ANNIE: We'll take a moment in silence to say goodbye to Sammy.

She takes the lid off the coffin – waits a moment – puts it back on angrily after rapping knuckles on coffin lid.

These things should not be allowed to happen. Children, I want you to understand, Sammy died from whooping cough and nothing could be done to save him. But that doesn't mean that more young lives should have to be wasted in this way. We shouldn't be afraid of death, it comes to us all, but it should come to the old, not to young people like yourselves. People used to be ignorant and believe that these things were sent us and nothing could be done to prevent them. But we are not ignorant any more, we know now that if people have warm, dry houses to live in, correct food to eat, proper medicine when they get ill and above all enough money to make sure that they can have those things – then there is no reason why these tragedies should continue. I want you to promise one thing today – and that is never to accept that nothing can be done. Always ask 'What can be done?' and when you find an answer, make sure it's done. Make sure it is done.

I would like a few moments on my own with Sam, so Ben, would you and the other children make your own way back to school.

They all go back to school where REVD. ELAND *is waiting – any pupils who had elected not to go would have already been spoken to by him – e.g. expressing surprise to find only them present; asking them where* MRS HIGDON *and the rest of the class were; asking them why they hadn't gone and congratulating them on their sensible decision, etc.*

REVEREND: Stand up children. My, my, we are forgetting our manners this morning aren't we?! Good morning children. (*He repeats this if they don't respond first time.*) Be seated. And what's the meaning of this? Where have you all been? Well . . .?

He gets their response.

Ah yes, Sammy Phillips who died most unfortunately last night.

The remainder of the scene was improvised around the following points and structure to allow for the young people's own responses and contributions.

Areas Covered: Were you made to go? What do you mean you had a choice? So why did you go? Can be repeated by several children individually.

REVEREND (*improvised*): But I'm sure you'd agree with me children that you only went because your teacher asked you to! Children always do as they're told! Why couldn't you go at the end of school to pay your respects?
And were your parents consulted?
So you think you're old enough to be able to make such decisions for yourselves? How do you know you're making the right choice or decision?
Now you've been to see Sammy I take it you're going to lie awake at night, afraid, frightened of dying?
This is ridiculous, you've wasted a whole morning. A whole morning in which you've learnt nothing. Have you learnt anything? What?

They talk about the cause(s) of Sammy's death — about learning not just to accept things, about not being afraid of death. The Reverend dismisses any notion that Sammy died because of poor living conditions, e.g. His parents work don't they? They get a wage don't they? So they can do what they want with it. They could either choose to spend it all in the ale house or choose to save some of it for a rainy day.

REVEREND: Children, I'm not here to argue with you. It's not your fault you're thinking like this.
What were those that stayed behind meant to be doing?
Do you think that children can be trusted to be left on their own?
So where is Mrs Higdon now? You know what happens when children are left on their own? They get up to mischief, they misbehave . . .

ANNIE *returns.*

REVEREND: Ah! Mrs Higdon!

ANNIE: Yes, Reverend?

REVEREND: I want a word with you about the way you and your husband are educating these children . . .

CO-ORDINATOR: Freeze.

Headlines: Vicar telling teachers off in front of their class?
Children being left unattended in the classroom?
Teachers taking children to see dead bodies without their parents' permission.

CO-ORDINATOR: What have you discovered there to help our investigation? . . . Relax. (*They exit.*)

Sample Questions:
Why did the Revd. Eland disapprove of the school outing? Do you think that young people of your age are too young to be learning about death? Are there any things you're too young to learn about? What? Why would you want to learn about that? Should you have been given a choice? Do you have a say in what goes on in your school? Would you like to? What would you do that was different?

4 Late Night Lesson

Characters: Annie Higdon   – Headteacher
                 Marjory Brandon
                 Ben Philpotts   Pupils

Setting: On the village green – late on a summer's evening.

Form: Combination of scripted theatre and participatory drama. The children are in role as the Burston school pupils throughout this scene. The Co-ordinator sets up the context (including the information that all the children's parents have given permission for them to attend this 'late night lesson'). The drama starts when Annie Higdon calls all the pupils onto the Green.

ANNIE: Come along children, everyone onto the Green. Sit down children. (*She sits.*) I must have a chair. (BEN *volunteers.*) Thank you Ben. (*He puts it beside her.*) This is a beautiful evening. Tonight, as the sky begins to darken we will have our first late-night lesson the Green. What will we learn? (*She looks round the group.*) Look up. Can you see? There and there. The precursors of the night world. The first light of two stars to reach us this evening. There's another and another, there too. Soon the sky will reveal the truth – we are a tiny world in a vast universe, and it will become clearer to us as darkness falls and all the stars are illuminated. (*She brings her attention back from the heavens to them.*) Well! Everyone ever born on this earth has seen those stars. There are more stars out there than people alive on this earth now; more numbers of stars even than all the people who have lived and died on our earth for the whole of its history. More stars than anyone can ever count. If you were set the task of counting them tonight it would be a task that you could not finish in the whole of your life, even if you spent your whole life counting, 1, 2, 3, 4, 5, 6, 7. Not stopping for tea or supper or sleep. 8, 9, 10, 11, 12, 13, 14, and still there would be more. Hundreds and thousands and millions more. We can't see them all tonight but one day in the future we will have a telescope powerful enough and then we will look out past the great galaxy of Orion and the Horse's Head into the depths of space and then you will see that we are such a tiny world in a vast universe. But for tonight we do have a telescope – a small one – loaned to us by Mrs Boulton at the shop, her father's brother was a sailor. (*She produces it.*) Mrs Boulton's telescope. Of course she didn't invent it. It was first invented in Holland in 1608. (*She looks through the telescope.*) One of the first people to use it to look at the heavens was a man called Galileo.

BEN: Gally who, Mrs Higdon?

ANNIE: Somebody help Ben. (*He gets help.*) That is correct. Galileo lived in Italy and when he looked through his telescope, what he saw astonished him. For it was the opposite of what people then thought to be true. Have you ever sat in a train at a station looking out of the window at another train and thought the other train was moving? Then when you looked out of the other window at the platform you discovered that you were moving, not the other train. The opposite of what you thought. Well, Galileo's discovery was as clear as that to him, and they threw him in prison.

MARJORY: Why?

ANNIE: Exactly — Why? That's what we're going to look at. We're going to look at what everyone thought to be true before Galileo looked through his telescope.

Can everyone move to the edge of the Green: this chair is the earth. (*Places it in centre of Green.*) Now we need some of the planets that are in our solar system. Can anyone name a planet? (*Gets responses.*) Come and stand here and be . . . (*Gets three children up to be three planets.*) Now we need the sun. (BEN *volunteers.*) Ben, can you be the sun for us? Now we need someone to come and sit on the earth. Now 400 years ago who would a lot of people think to be the most important person on earth? (*If they don't mention the Pope then include:*) Someone else who people thought was very important was the head of the church, the Pope — can I have a volunteer to be the Pope? Pope, I want you to look out from the earth and then tell us all what you see.

Planets and the sun, look how far away from the earth you are. Circle slowly around the earth, keeping the same distance from it. Begin . . . Stop.

Pope, what did you see? (*Get response and then ask that pupil to return to the edge of the Green.*) That's what people thought to be true before Galileo. Like the person in the train who looked out of one window and thought the train next to them was moving, so the people on the earth thought the other planets and the sun were moving and the earth was standing still. Galileo wasn't content to just look out of one window: he realised there was another way of looking at it. All of you are going to be Galileo and we'll see what he discovered. This time, planets, I want you to circle round the sun: watch carefully what happens. Begin. . . Stop. What have you discovered? (*Get responses.*) That's what Galileo discovered — that all the planets including the earth in our solar system circled round the *sun*, not the earth. And they threw him in prison for that!

MARJORY: }
BEN: } Why?

Question and Answer session between Annie Higdon and the pupils.

Underlying Aims:
1   To explore the notion of change and resistance to change.
2   To challenge the notion of 'important people' always being right.
3   To encourage the pupils to think about the 'order of things' in the village of Burston.

After the Question and Answer session:

ANNIE: Children, you have worked very hard tonight. These are difficult questions we have been considering and I have found it most stimulating, but rather tiring. So, because I am interested in all our minds being ready and awake to tackle more difficult problems tomorrow, I think it is time you all ran along home to bed. Off you go now.

CO-ORDINATOR: Freeze.

Headlines: Children having lessons outside, late at night, without books or slates and chalk?
Teachers teaching children that important people can be wrong?
Children learning that things don't always have to stay the same?

CO-ORDINATOR: What have we discovered there to help our investigation? Relax . . .

Sample Questions:
What would the school managers have to say about this lesson? Would they be upset? Why? Why couldn't Mrs Higdon have taught the children about the stars and Galileo in the classroom on the blackboard? How useful/important is that lesson for the farmworkers' children in Burston? Why do you think people found Galileo's discoveries upsetting? What's the order of things in Burston? What was it like to be in Mrs Higdon's class? What was she like as a teacher?

5 Grandad Goes to School

Characters: Albert Brandon — Marjory's grandfather and guardian
Marjory Brandon — Senior pupil
Tom Higdon — Assistant teacher

Setting: Albert's and Marjory's farmworkers cottage.

Form: Presentational scripted theatre.

TOM HIGDON (*reading letter*): He says he wants to put the rent up by three pence a week. So what do we say in reply, Mr Brandon?

ALBERT: I can't afford it. Not unless I'm paid more.

TOM: Good. We don't want to waste words. How shall we start?

MARJORY: 'Dear Sir'.

ALBERT: I never could use one of these. (*Indicates pen.*)

MARJORY: It's like this Grandad. (*Demonstrates.*) Don't press so hard. (MARJORY *shows her slate reading 'Dear Sir'.*)

ALBERT: I see she been learning off you then, Tom. Learning to write good as well. Fair disgrace me, I bet.

TOM: But they're your words. Your words! Even though they're hard to write. (*Pause.*) So what's next?

ALBERT: I been paying no more rent.

MARJORY: I'm writing to say I cannot afford to pay any more rent.

ALBERT: Since me wages is too low.

TOM: Especially since your son has gone up to London. You help him, Marjory.

ALBERT: Who said 'helpless as a child'? Should say 'helpless as a man who can't write'.

TOM: Know why they want to put the rents up all round? 'Cos of labourers starting unions. Labourers ask for better wages and farmers don't want to lose on it. So they put the rents up.

ALBERT: Put that in, shall I?

TOM: They don't like working men too smart. Now remember: Farmer Fisher may say no. Can you start putting a few pennies by?

ALBERT: No. I'm going to fight. You said I should!

TOM: We'll win the big fight when it comes. Sign it! Now, read it back.

ALBERT: 'Dear Sir, I am writing to say I cannot afford any more rent since my wages is too low. Also my son is now gone up to London.
Yours sincerely, Albert Brandon.'

MARJORY: How many marks?

TOM: How many would you say, Marjory?

MARJORY: I should say: Full marks!

CO-ORDINATOR: Freeze . . .

Headlines: Teachers interfering in other people's business?
Children showing up their grandparents?
Teachers encouraging workers to complain to their landlords?

CO-ORDINATOR: What have you discovered there to help our investigation? Relax . . . actors.

Sample Questions:
Why did Albert need to write a letter? Wouldn't it have been easier if Tom or Marjory had written it for him? Why didn't they? What does he need to learn to write for? Isn't he too old? Why was Tom encouraging Albert to fight? Why was Tom interfering in things that were none of his business? What's Grandad's rent got to do with a schoolteacher?

6 Sharpening the Sickle

Characters: Tom Higdon   Assistant teacher
Bet Phillips
George Letts   Farmworkers

Setting: In the fields.

Form: Scripted presentational theatre leading into participatory drama.

GEORGE: Who's this now?

BET: Tom Higdon on his travels by the looks of it.

TOM (*entering*): George, Bet. I see you got some work on then.

GEORGE: On holiday again?

TOM: Yes. Been over at Diss. Union matters.

BET: I heard you was on the union side of things.

TOM: You coming to the meeting?

BET: What's it for?

TOM: Labourers want to start a union branch here in Burston.

GEORGE: Make yourself unpopular, you will.

BET: Not with me. Teach my Alice good, don't you, Tom? Always got her head in a book.

TOM: Try as we can, Bet.

BET: So what I be wanting a union for?

TOM: Put a sharpness on that sickle of yours. Put a decent wage in your hand. Last week, at Stetford, union put two pence on the wage of every worker on the estate.

GEORGE: Farmers won't like that.

TOM: They got no choice. Farmers don't want justice. We have to take it.

GEORGE: And how'll you do that?

TOM: By every man and woman joining the union. Which is why I want to see you tonight, George, at Barney's.

GEORGE: You'll see me all right. If you look outa Barney's window you can see right into the pub. That's where I'll be!

BET: I've heard you complainin' often enough, an' talkin' about changes what are needed aroun' here.

GEORGE: They won't allow it.

BET: Don't mind him. (*She starts to bang the handle of her sickle on the ground.*)

TOM: Let me see that. Handle's dangerous. I've known these come off, go through a worker's leg. Mr Fisher should be payin' for this.

BET: Yeah, when the stars come down from the sky.

TOM: Reach up an' take 'em, Bet, reach up an' take 'em. I'll see you tonight then? (*Hands her a leaflet and starts to leave.*)

BET: I expect.

GEORGE: What's he given yer? (GEORGE *comes over.*)

CO-ORDINATOR: Freeze.
   What's in that leaflet Tom has given to Bet? (*Get responses.*)
   Relax . . . actors.
   So Tom is organising a meeting for the farmworkers to discuss whether or not they want a union.

Brief Question and Answer session around the following areas:
What is a union? What sort of problems could a union help to tackle for the farm labourers? Why was George worried about the union?

CO-ORDINATOR: It would be useful for our investigation to explore what might have happened at that meeting. In order to do that I need to ask if you would be the farm labourers. Will you do that? Remember it's different from being the pupils of Burston school. This time we are asking you to be the parents of those children, the adults in the village.

(The forging of this contract and the preparation for the drama is dependent on the needs of the particular class.)

The Union Meeting
(The Union Meeting is a follow-on and continuation of **Sharpening the Sickle**. They are not separate scenes in the investigation.)

Characters: Tom Higdon   Assistant teacher
            Bet Phillips
            George Letts   Farmworkers
            Peggy May (played by Co-ordinator for this section)

Setting: Barney's workshop, after work.

Form: Scripted opening followed by improvised drama.

CO-ORDINATOR: We're now going to join a meeting that Tom Higdon called to see whether people in Burston were interested in starting a branch of the Farmworkers' Union. Now a lot of people went to that meeting, so that's why we're asking you to put yourselves in the shoes of those farmworkers, so that we've got a lot of people at the meeting as well, so that we can discover things that happened there.

Some of the people that went to the meeting – like George (*indicating him*) – weren't really very sure about setting up a union. They didn't think that it would be allowed to happen. Other people thought like Bet. (*Indicates her.*) They were very interested in setting up a union. It might help to sort things out. Other people had different opinions. I shall be at the meeting too. My name is Peggy and I'm a farmworker in Burston. The drama will start just before Tom Higdon comes to speak to the meeting.

TOM (*entering*): 'Ere – sorry I'm late . . . Good . . .! I never expected to see so many of you, that's tremendous . . . George, so you changed your mind then!

GEORGE: We'll see how the meeting goes, Tom.

TOM: Good, George, I'm pleased . . . (*Goes round circle naming individual young people.*) Look, thanks very much everyone of you. I know you've all been working very hard today in the fields and you've got to be up again early in the morning, so thank you for turning up here at Barney's.

This meeting, as you're all aware, as I've been cycling round the fields during me school holidays with these leaflets, is to make a decision as to whether we're going to start a branch of the new Farmworkers' Union here in Burston, or not. (*He goes to squeeze onto one of the benches.*) . . . 'Ere, move along a little bit . . . thanks. So who here thinks there are things in our village which are not right, things which are not fair in our village that need changing? (*Responses.*) . . . A lot of you – let's share some of the things that's wrong; I know you've all got experiences to share – friends or family or something that's happened to yourselves, so let's share it . . .

An improvised Question and Answer session followed in which the four A/Ts contributed conflicting views when appropriate to further and deepen the thoughts and feelings the young people were articulating; a selection of points and questions used is therefore included:

1   How many other people here have had experience of having their rents put up?
2   Do you know of anyone who's been hurt or injured by faulty tools? Can you tell us who it was, was it a friend of yours? What happened to her – for those who don't know? . . . So she got cut – badly – was she able to go to work? . . . (TOM)

This sort of thing happens all the time; it's their fault for not looking after their tools; they're our tools to look after, aren't they? . . . (GEORGE)

So it's important that we buy our own tools, like we've always done? You're agreeing with George, yes? (PEGGY)

New machines? As long as there's still work for us when they get them.

3   What do you think's wrong with our jobs at the moment? (BET)

It's too hard work? Yes it is. (BET)

It seems to me that you want everything your own way. You want more money for less work; you want the farmers to buy this and do that; what are you going to do for yourselves then? . . . It's too easy. (GEORGE)

Well, let's hear from those people who've got worries, like George . . . we've already heard from over there, about the way we've always bought our own tools, other people who've got worries . . . yes, go on . . . (TOM)

4   Oh, so you're getting — (rats, leaks/damp, etc.) in your house? . . . they're in such a bad state of repair . . . they're not good enough — well, what can the union do about this? (TOM) Anyone got any suggestions as to how starting a branch of the union here in Burston can help with these things?

They got tuppence on their wages in Stetford by starting a union. (BET) I don't know quite what they did to get it tho' . . .

I know people in Stetford who don't like to have anything to do with the union . . . 'cos if you join the union you're causing trouble. (GEORGE)

5   Well there's a lot of suggestions coming up now, so why don't we talk about them amongst ourselves to find out what everyone here thinks. Just take a couple of minutes talking to the people next to you about whether we should start the union here in Burston or not . . . (TOM)

6   All right then, I'm sorry I'm going to have to stop all this discussion. There's a lot of points being made, so let's call the meeting back to order and share them. Let's hear from . . . etc. etc. (TOM)

7   We've heard from Bet and . . . and . . . and . . . and other people that now is the time to start the union. We've heard from George and . . . and . . . and . . . and other people that now is not the time to start the union. So now is the time to make up your minds, each and every one of you. Those of you who think that now is not the time, go and stand over there, and those of you who think that now is the time, go and stand over here. Those of you who are still not sure, stay here in the middle.

CO-ORDINATOR: Freeze . . . and hold it there . . . I want you to think whilst you're standing there whether it was an easy decision for you to make or a difficult one . . . if it was easy, what were the things that made it easy? If it was difficult, what were the things that made it difficult? And what does your decision and other people's decisions mean — not just for you but for the whole village? Has everyone decided the same thing?
And carry on with the drama.

TOM, BET and PEGGY continue to discuss with the young people the implications of their own and other people's decisions. Those who have not made up their minds are questioned and urged to do so. GEORGE is against the union and leaves quietly. This actor/teacher then re-enters as FARMER STERNE. His contribution is not scripted but covers the following points:

FARMER STERNE:
1   What is this meeting about?

2   What is a teacher doing at a meeting of farmworkers?

3   Who is joining this union and who is not? (Those who are unsure are encouraged to decide, e.g. 'I should advise you to make up your mind — are you for this union or not — and don't forget who gives you a job and a house while you're making that decision.'

4   You realise the sort of problems a union is going to cause? (FARMER STERNE outlines his own economic difficulties, the benefits of a patriarchical system, the generations over which this 'family' system has worked perfectly well, the divisions and pain that troublemakers can cause. He asks what they would do in his position.)

During this intervention TOM challenges FARMER STERNE making clear his own position and enabling the pupils in role to develop further understandings of their rights and their power.

5   I want to make one thing quite clear, there will be no union on my land and anybody who thinks otherwise may find themselves without a job and that means without a house.

6   Now I want to have a quiet word with you people who have shown a bit of common sense and don't want this union. Who organised this meeting? Who spoke up a lot in favour of it? Come up to the farmhouse and we'll have a chat.

CO-ORDINATOR: Freeze.

Headlines: Farmworkers working for the same farmer, doing the same job, but disagreeing?
A farmer threatening his workers?
A teacher involved with a farmworkers' union?

CO-ORDINATOR: What have we discovered to help our investigation?
    Relax.

Sample Questions:
What's a teacher got to do with a farmworkers' union? Isn't he just interfering? What was your attitude to the union? Why? Why was Farmer Sterne so determined to stop a union being formed? Some people decided not to join the union. Who were they helping?

The Fruits of the Investigation:
During the final small group discussion, the pupils are asked to identify what they think are the real underlying reasons for the dismissal of the teachers. They are encouraged to examine the links between the different events in order to avoid over-simplification into a single 'answer'.

While links to their own education and experience should be made throughout the day, it is particularly valuable at this point to ask the pupils to reflect on who decides what should be taught to them. Has what they have been doing today been education?

Having drawn together the threads of the first part of the investigation and looked back at their original ideas as to why the teachers were dismissed, the investigation moves on to examine what happened after the dismissal. The heart of this section is the continuation of Dossy's story, which is fully scripted. However, the script is designed either to be presented in full at the end of the investigation or, if time and the needs of the pupils demand it, to be stopped at certain points enabling further participatory exploration by the group. Thus, the programme can contract or expand: it is responsive to the pupils. The remaining script is therefore reproduced in full with asterisks and letters indicating possible intervention points. The purpose and form of these inserted participation sessions are explained after Dossy's speech.

Dossy's Story continued

DOSSY: You know what I did when I heard Mr and Mrs Higdon had been dismissed? That's right – I cried, and Marjory say 'We're going to do something about this'. Well, she did. She went right up to the blackboard and wrote on it – 'We're going on strike.' That's when I stopped a crying. I was shocked I can tell you. 'Going on strike? We can't.' 'You just have', she say and turned the blackboard over so it faced the wall. 'When them new teachers get into this classroom tomorrow, they'll know they ain't wanted. We want Mr and Mrs Higdon back, they're our teachers.' Tha's when I smiled, I suppose I thought that was that. They'll see it an go away an then we'll carry on like before all this business. My sister Marjory were nothing if she weren't clear-headed. 'Hide that board rubber and then come along with me,' she say.

'Cos all the village was buzzing with the news. Mrs Boulton's shop were full. Marjory went onto the Green and marched up to Ben who were playing five stones. She grabbed hold o' him and say 'You tell all the children we're going on strike in the morning.' He smiled. Then he was off. She just stood there on the Green and waited. It were Gladys Sturman who got there first – she come on her mother's bike ringing the bell and shouting 'Strike, strike, strike.' She were a nice girl Gladys. (*There is a moment as* DOSSY *remembers* GLADYS – *now dead*.) Then they was all there – Henry Gotts, Eddie Higgins, Henry Ling, Violet Mulinger, Frank Durbridge, not the Philpott sisters, they was too scared. But 70 out of the 80 of us kids were there and Marjory got on Gladys's mum's bike and shouted – 'Are we all going on strike?' and we all shouted – 'Yes'. That always make me cry. But Marjory she went straight on. 'Right then we gotta get organised.' She were like a general. 'Gladys' – 'Yes Marjory' – 'Get everyone to sign their names, in joined-up writing.' That got a cheer 'cos it meant she thought we were all grown up even the little uns. 'We're going to need a banner, Henry Gotts you can do that.' He were good at drawing, she knew what was what did that sister o' mine. 'I want everybody here early. Go and get your parents for a meeting on the Green.' So thas what we did (*Intervention A*). We was up till 12 o'clock, little uns an all. Nobody went to bed early. An all our parents said 'Yes we're going to support you.' Nex' day we was all out here in front o' the school, nobody felt tired, and we all got banners and placards and the drum, and the accordion, an' we marched round singing an shouting – we're on strike. They had police an all sorts, but that didn't bother us. We weren't going to school till we got our teachers back. But the Managers weren't having it. So we stopped out on strike. Then Mr and Mrs Higdon started giving us our lessons on the Green. We called it our School on the Green. I was happy again. Then two weeks into the strike we found out how determined they were we weren't going to win. All the parents of the children on strike got a letter with a stamp – posted in Norwich. Something was up. Our parents was being prosecuted for keeping us away from school. They all gotta go to court. That made my mother think twice I can tell you . . . (*Intervention B*). But all the parents and the older children, they marched together up to Norwich, singing songs and chanting. And they was fined a quarter of a week's wages (2/6d.) for their trouble.

A/T: Do you think they gave up the strike after that? No. The children kept going to the School on the Green, kept fighting for a proper education. And when the weather got bad they moved their school into the carpenter's shop. Then all the parents received another summons and this time they were fined half a week's wages (5/-). But they wouldn't give up their fight. They marched to and from the Norwich court house singing their songs and rattling collecting tins.

DOSSY: And the money started coming in, not just from Norfolk people, but as the news spread through the trade union movement, money come in from working people in London, Scotland, Manchester, Wales — from all over. Until we'd collected enough money not just to pay Mr and Mrs Higdon regular like but enough money to build a proper school — the Burston Strike School. Cor, that were a special day that were. Three years after the strike started, on a hot day in May 1917, two thousand people were crammed onto the Green (that's five times as many people as actually lived in the village). There was singing and dancing and speeches and cheering and up at the front was my sister Marjory. She stood there between Mr and Mrs Higdon and it were Marjory who cut through the thick red ribbon across the door and declared the Burston Strike School open.

A/T: And for 25 years the school was there, run by Annie and Tom Higdon. For 25 years those children and in turn their children went to the Strike School. Until in 1939 Tom Higdon died and seven years later Annie Higdon also died.

DOSSY: As a long time ago, seventy years. They're both dead now, Mr and Mrs Higdon. He died first. She lived on her own in the village. I often used to see her out walking. 'Morning Mrs Higdon', I'd say. 'Morning Mrs Wynne' she'd say. I'd watch her walking up the road, she got a bit o' arthritis in one leg, but she were a fighter. I'd watch her and I'd think: 'If it weren't for you and people like you, governess, my gran'children'd still be working in them fields an wouldn't know no better.' She an' that Mr Higdon they were fighters, an' they knew whose side they were on — the side of us working people.

A/T *takes off* DOSSY's *hat.*

A/T: And those are some of the things that Dossy and the other people in the village told us about the years after the village children went on strike . . . When we went to Burston we visited Tom and Annie's graves. Someone had placed flowers and this poem there . . .
'Some pity the farmers, but I tell you now,
Pity poor labourers that follow the plough,
Pity poor children half starving and thin,
Divide every great farm into ten.'

*

Intervention A

The Parent's Meeting: A drama role play in which the children are the parents of the Burston School children. They have to decide whether or not to support the strike initiated by the children. The key question to be addressed is what is so special about the education offered by the Higdons? What makes it worth fighting for?

Underlying Aims:
1   To enable the pupils to explore more deeply the questions:
    What is education?
    What is it for?
    Who controls it and for whose benefit?
2   To enable the pupils to use and develop understandings gained through the process of the investigation in a concrete way.

3 To reveal more clearly the conflicting needs of the farmers/School Managers and the labourers.
4 To explore the potential strength of collective action.

Intervention B

The Court: A drama role play in which the children are the parents of the Burston School children. Each parent has received a summons. Their decision is whether or not to continue the fight. Their task, after some preparation, is to present their case to the magistrate. The key questions to be addressed are why are the School Managers, the farmers and the law so determined to stop the Higdons teaching the labourers' children? What do they want/need education to be like?

Underlying Aims:
These are the same as for Intervention A, with the addition of:
5 To explore the role of the legal system in relation to the different educational needs of farmworkers and farmers and School Managers.

The more structured nature of the Court was more appropriate for some groups than the looser role play of the Parents' Meeting on the Green. Other forms and other points of intervention can be and were used.

The core of the programme is Dossy's story and the investigation. Any company using this script would need to develop their own approaches within that framework according to their own skills and the needs of the pupils.

QUESTIONS ARISING IN 1985 FROM A MUTINY IN 1789

Devised by Action PIE

Written by Geoff Gillham
For Secondary Pupils

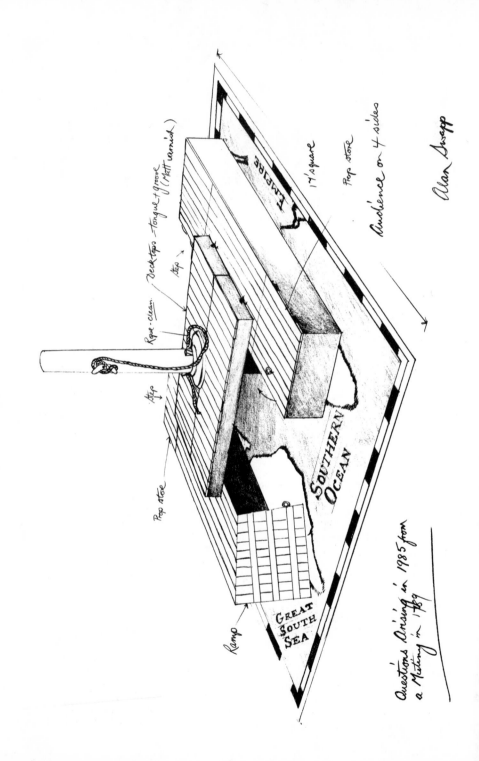

EMPIRE

17' square

Prop store

Audience on 4 sides

Deck tops - tongue + groove (Matt varnish)

step →

Rope - clean

step

step

Prop store

SOUTHERN OCEAN

GREAT SOUTH SEA

Ramp

Questions Arising in 1985 from a Meeting in 1789

Alan Snapp

QUESTIONS ARISING IN 1985 FROM A MUTINY IN 1789

The origin of *Questions Arising* . . . lies very much in the great miners' strike of 1984–5. The members of Action Projects in Education based in Cardiff and on the edge of the South Wales Coalfield not only gave their full support to the strike, but felt it extremely important to understand and analyse its development from the standpoint of getting rid of the Thatcher government. It was clear from the earliest stages that neither the miners nor the National Coal Board/State were going to give way; and that therefore the strike was implicitly a struggle for power.

The idea of writing a play about the mutiny on the *Bounty* had been with me for several years. It was under the conditions of the miners' strike that it pushed itself forward, sensuously, demanding as it were 'write about me *now*'. Yet, contradictorily, I didn't do so by the company's deadline. Instead, I had found myself more and more actively involved in political work in the Kent Coalfield. In addition, the richness, complexity, and superabundance of relevant themes which emerged as I researched the subject was very daunting.

As a result the play was really group devised, with me leading the process as director. About ten days before we opened, I stopped rehearsal and wrote the play in about three days. The important thing here is that the play (and the programme as a whole) was created in a crucible which is expressed in the full title. We approached the factual material and accounts of the mutiny intuitively – our path through it and the questions determined by our struggle to understand the movement of the miners' strike. But the play is in no way a crude allegory, nor has the factual material been distorted to fit a thesis. (It is closer to known historical fact than any of the three films on the subject.) On the contrary, we have tried in the manner of scientists to analyse the mutiny (using for tools our basic knowledge of human behaviour, motivation etc.) as 'Other' of the whole political situation in Britain. One may compare this activity to that of the Polish film director Andrej Wajda who threw himself into the making of *Danton* after the declaration of martial law in December 1981.

It will be noticed from what I have said that the pupils were not the starting point. This may seem a heresy to child-centred educators. It may seem instead that we have started from our (political) views. This impression might be confirmed at first sight by the text which certainly has a didactic form. Some adults who saw the play in performance indeed took strong exception to the play precisely on these grounds. They 'didn't like being told what to think at the ends of the scenes'. They wanted to have 'their own thoughts'. I haven't the space to deal specifically with the significance of this reaction but I would point the interested reader to Walter Benjamin's essay on Brecht's epic theatre published in *Standing Conference of Young People's Theatre Journal 13* (pp. 31–2). It may be of use to elaborate here my (and Action PIE's) theoretical approach to TIE, and theatre and education in general.

We start with *the world about us* which of course is about young people too. Our job as artists is to struggle to understand *it* and then to create a sensuous representation of it, which enables others (the pupils) to understand it. Understanding is a process. One can understand nothing without the process of understanding. The process is learning; the product is knowledge (however incomplete). We can *know* about the way people behave and interact, why historical events occur in the way they do in precisely the same way as we can know about, say, how photo-synthesis works in plants. All that is required (which is a lot admittedly!) is to study the phenomenon itself and to develop intellectual tools to do so. This is what education should comprise. Art is not about views therefore. There is a body of knowledge which is the province of art, and especially of theatre. This concerns the workings of human consciousness, the activity and development of human beings, and the processes of society as a whole particularly as manifested in individuals.

Art is in this sense always didactic. *Questions Arising . . .*, like Brecht's plays, only makes this property of art explicit. The false barriers between art and science are torn away. The pupils are asked to observe a phenomenon, a scientific experiment, and then to grapple with it, to understand and abstract the objective laws of human behaviour as they pertain (in this case) to how people come to rebellion.

Questions Arising . . . is not child-centred in the sense of starting from or dealing with the direct experience of young people. It is teacher-centred. We accept responsibility as teachers for deciding what the class needs to learn about, and for structuring the learning material in an appropriate and 'beguiling' way, to use Dorothy Heathcote's phrase.[1] As teachers we offer this, on the face of it, distant material but we 'render it worth knowing, which means to make knowledge gained usable in one's own thinking beyond the situation in which the learning has occurred' (J.S. Bruner).[2]

How does this method manifest itself in *Questions Arising . . .*? The recent riots in Birmingham, London and elsewhere demonstrate that young people are headed towards 'mutiny'. What they want and need to know is how to *win*. The subject of the play provides them with an opportunity to work out how to win, although not in the form of a blueprint. The material is there but the pupil must do the active work of understanding. The play 'beguiles' because all the relations on the *Bounty* are a replica of the relations in a school: pupils/crew; teachers/officers; head teacher/captain. This is never explicit. The replication functions as secondary hidden symbolism: third year secondary school pupils know only too well those crisis assemblies when the Head calls the whole school together after a particularly shameful piece of behaviour by a few pupils – echoed in the dynamics of the coconut scene. Or the liberal teacher trying to get to the bottom of a 'mindless' act of vandalism – echoed in the Brown/Nelson scene. The simultaneous distance and closeness of these scenes is what fuels the pupils' desire to understand, and empowers them to do so. The same process applies to the sexual ambivalences embedded in the play and production, for an age-range that is preoccupied with sorting out sexuality, love, friendship and comradeship. The statements that follow each scene emerge then not as moral homilies, but as scientific abstractions which either invite in pupils the simple question – 'is that so?', or which encapsulate what they have already intuitively grasped from the scene itself.

A note on production: The Action PIE production was performed by two men and two women. No attempt was made to 'disguise' this. The actors wore comfortable present-day clothes mainly in creams and dark blues but without any attempt beyond this to 'nauticalise' them. They are themselves, showing how people behave. At the end of scenes, the freezes are not technical devices. They are what Dorothy Heathcote calls 'depictions' and should be consciously worked at to distil the essence of the moment set against the closing narration. In the breaks after each scene, the young people were invited to chat with each other while prop changes took place. Actors here changed their costume signs (sailors' square scarfs for crew, epaulettes for officers, captain's hat for Bligh) and identity signs (knife for Churchill, snake-bag for Muspratt etc.) and 'mutiny-relation' badges.

The workshop that followed the play recreated characters' actions from the play at the class's choice. The pupils then discussed, interrogated the character, speculated on occasions in group work, facilitating themselves. By 'facilitating', I mean functioning as a teacher, structuring and focussing the interaction between the class and the actor/teacher in role or character. The fact that the play set them all up *as actors* (rather than characters) made this particularly comfortable for pupils and actors alike.

Because of time and personnel limitations, Action PIE did not produce a teachers' pack for the first run. We would have done so for a second run. Cockpit however did so. Their pack contained extracts from the play and discussion points, and a selection of photographs for use by teachers as stimulus material for later classroom work.

A note on Action PIE

Questions Arising . . . was first performed in February 1985. Action PIE had its grant withdrawn by South Glamorgan Education Authority in December 1985. The Authority's stated reasons were that the company's work was of poor quality and irrelevant to the needs of young people. The Welsh Arts Council and the South East Wales Arts Association also withdrew their funding, stating they 'did not dissent from that view'. None of the Labour Councillors concerned in the cutting of funds had seen the work of the company in schools. Officers from WAC and SEWAA refused Action PIE's request to amplify or explain their statements.

Equity Council, the actors' union, at first officially supported the company in its demand for re-funding. On March 4th 1986 they abandoned Action PIE, having taken no action whatsoever to defend the company.

Geoff Gillham

1 Dorothy Heathcote, noted thinker and practitioner in Drama in Education. See *Dorothy Heathcote — Collected Writings on Education and Drama,* ed. by L. Johnson and C. O'Neill (Hutchinson, 1984).

2 J.S. Bruner, educational psychologist. His writings on the structuring of learning include *Towards A Theory of Instruction* (Harvard, 1966) and *The Relevance of Education* (George Allen and Unwin, 1971).

Questions Arising in 1985 from a Mutiny in 1789 was first performed in South Glamorgan schools on 12 February 1985 by Action PIE, with the following cast:

NARRATOR	Shared among all actors
WILLIAM BLIGH	Caroline Stubbs
FLETCHER CHRISTIAN (*Midshipman*)	Marcelle Davies
CHURCHILL (*Able Seaman*)	Gary McComb
BROWN (*Able Seaman*)	Jan Koene
BURKITT (*Able Seaman*)	Jan Koene
COLEMAN (*Armourer*)	Caroline Stubbs
MUSPRATT (*Able Seaman*)	Marcelle Davies
EDWARD YOUNG (*Midshipman*)	Gary McComb
FRYER (*Ship's Master*)	Marcelle Davies
LEBROGUE (*Sailmaker*)	Gary McComb
DAVID NELSON (*Botanist*)	Caroline Stubbs
QUINTAL (*Able Seaman*)	Jan Koene

Written by Geoff Gillham
Directed by Geoff Gillham
Designed by Alan Swapp

The present script is a revised version, prepared for the production by Cockpit TIE company.

NARRATION: This play was written in 1985 during the miners' strike. It is called *Questions Arising in 1985 from a Mutiny in 1789*. The questions remain. (*Pause.*) Nearly two hundred years ago, a small sailing ship left Portsmouth for the Pacific. Its objective was to collect bread-fruit plants in Tahiti and transport them to the West Indies, where they were to be planted as a staple food crop for slaves. The ship never reached Jamaica; nor did it return to England. Although at this time, the loss of a ship was not unusual, because of the circumstances of its loss, this ship became one of the most notorious in naval history. Its name was the *Bounty*. It was lost not because of storms, shipwreck or disease; but because its crew seized the *Bounty* from the captain by force.

Depiction of the Mutiny: BLIGH *stands in a launch, facing away from the ship.* CHURCHILL *is holding a musket, relaxed and looks towards* BLIGH. CHRISTIAN *stands by the mooring point, cutlass in hand. Disturbed.*

NARRATION: They put him in a launch with those who opposed the mutiny, and sailed the ship to an unknown island. And there the ship was destroyed. (*Hold.*)

CHRISTIAN *in mental pain cries 'Go-o-o' as he brings his cutlass down on the mooring line from the ship to* BLIGH's *launch. The* NARRATOR, *as* BROWN, *holds an imaginary helm, and looks straight ahead. Hold.*

We are not concerned with *why* the mutiny happened. That much is clear — conditions were intolerable. Fifty men cooped up for over two years with little space; food that a dog would refuse; working conditions more dangerous even than those of miners; a captain whose over-riding intention was to fulfil the aims of the voyage, no matter what it cost. But, really, there was nothing unusual in all this. No. It is more a matter of why there weren't mutinies on every ship! The questions we are asking are these: What did it feel like to *be* in a mutiny? How do people *get* to mutiny? What problems are people faced with on the way to doing it and when they've done it? These are the questions arising in 1985 from a mutiny in 1789 — the year of the French Revolution, that toppled a dictatorial government and began a new era in man's struggle for freedom, equality and brotherhood.

NARRATION: Break.

Depiction breaks. The actors prepare for the next scene.

We shall play many parts. All the people really existed but we have invented their characters. Each will wear a badge. Red for mutineer. Blue for non-mutineer. To show you at all times what he does not know himself until he does it. No one knows exactly how it was so we are not showing 'facts' in the narrow sense. In history, what is most interesting to future generations is rarely recorded!

But our job as actors is not the showing-of-facts, but imagining-the-real.

Depiction: CHURCHILL *is standing in the process of speaking, his finger pointing to the ground.* MUSPRATT *is kneeling looking to the space that* BURKITT *will occupy.* COLEMAN *is more inert but listening to the argument proceeding.* BURKITT *will join the depiction looking at* CHURCHILL *and about to speak.*

NARRATION: Question one. How did the crew see their situation before the *Bounty* left Portsmouth? Crew's quarters. Below decks. (BURKITT *joins the depiction.*)

BURKITT: That's what I'm saying! Everyone's been shifted to get them bloody plant racks in the Cabin area.

CHURCHILL: And who picks up the tab?!

BURKITT: We do.

CHURCHILL: What's going to happen if we get a dose of scurvy down here? This space we ain't got a chance. Go through like lightning. (MUSPRATT *is poking about to find some space.*) Get out of there Muspratt. That's mine. (MUSPRATT *retreats. Takes out his snake.*)

BURKITT: What do you think, Coleman?

COLEMAN (*to* MUSPRATT): What the hell have you got there?

MUSPRATT (*to all*): Snake.

BURKITT: Coleman.

COLEMAN: What?

BURKITT: I asked you a question.

COLEMAN (*still watching snake*): I think it's bad. What do you want us to say?

MUSPRATT: Burkitt, what am I going to do with Sloper? I ain't got . . .

COLEMAN: Eat it. Tastiest thing you'll get in two years.

CHURCHILL (*to* COLEMAN): What about the marines? Where are they supposed to go?

COLEMAN: Hanging over the side, what you think! There ain't any.

CHURCHILL: What!

BURKITT: Right that's it. Hear that Churchill? No marines.

CHURCHILL: Yeah.

BURKITT: First they coop us up in less space than they'd give to the chickens. To offset that they cut down on the crew — not on the officers mind —

CHURCHILL: Plenty of them!

BURKITT: — that means they're carrying less food. Now they expect us to do the fighting if we meet any savages.

MUSPRATT: We aren't gonna meet savages are we Burkitt?

BURKITT: Probably. (*No one says anything.*)

MUSPRATT: Sloper wouldn't like that.

CHURCHILL: No. Nor will you. (*Silence again.* CHURCHILL, BURKITT *and even* COLEMAN *brood on the situation.* MUSPRATT *handles the snake.*)

BURKITT: Alright lads, what we gonna do about it?! (*No response.*) Churchill?

CHURCHILL: What?

BURKITT: What do you mean 'what'? What are we going to do about it? (MUSPRATT *listens again.*)

CHURCHILL: Nothing we *can* do, is there?

BURKITT: Course there is!

CHURCHILL: What?

BURKITT: Go up and tell 'em we're not having it?

CHURCHILL: You must be joking. They don't listen to us.

BURKITT: No? A mate of mine was on the *Venus*. Someone found out the boats were rotten. They all went up and told the Captain they weren't leaving Bristol till there were proper boats and they got 'em. Double quick.

CHURCHILL: Yeah that was boats though.

BURKITT: Same difference. We go up there and tell 'em.

CHURCHILL: They won't listen to us.

BURKITT: They'll have to.

CHURCHILL: Don't you believe it. (*He sits back.*)

BURKITT: Look at you. Plenty of that (*gesture of chatting*) but when it comes to doing something you just sit back and take it.

CHURCHILL: *You* do something if you feel so strongly about it.

BURKITT: Oh yeah!

CHURCHILL: Yeah!

BURKITT: Look we're *all* in this. What's the use in just me going up! Coleman, Muspratt. We've all got to do it. Go up on me own, I'll just get marked down as a trouble-maker. Let's *do* something. Before we leave.

MUSPRATT: Yeah. Come on then. (*He doesn't move.*)

BURKITT (*ignoring* MUSPRATT): Coleman?

COLEMAN: No thanks.

BURKITT: Well that's just great, in it? Shout your mouths off, but no one wants to do anything.

COLEMAN: Why don't you get off your soap-box, Burkitt. You didn't have to come on this ship. It was your decision. No one press-ganged you. You don't like it, you go and tell him. Or just walk off again. We shan't miss you.

CHURCHILL: Oh shut up Coleman.

BURKITT: No. And no one's going to miss your trap if I put me boot in it.

COLEMAN (*shaping up*): You wanna try it?

MUSPRATT (*to* CHURCHILL): Is there going to be a fight?

BURKITT: Wouldn't waste my time. (*He looks to* CHURCHILL.)

CHURCHILL: They're too powerful, Burkitt. They've got all the aces. (*Pause.*)

MUSPRATT: Aren't we going to do anything?

BURKITT: No. It don't look like it. (*He stares at* CHURCHILL *and* COLEMAN.)

Depiction.

NARRATION: For a long time, people live under conditions they should not tolerate.

It is not that they *do* accept them:
But that they do not know they have the power to change them.

Break.

Depiction breaks. Change of stage properties.

Actors take up depiction for next scene: CHURCHILL *stands, his forehead against the mast. He holds his grog-mug in a limp hand.* BURKITT *sits, head in hands, tense.* COLEMAN *is lying down, grog-mug on his chest.*

Question two. How did the *Bounty*'s crew exist under the worst conditions? A man has died of pneumonia. He's just been buried at sea. The same men: Burkitt, Churchill and Coleman, the armourer.

COLEMAN: Once upon a time there was a healthy young lad called James Valentine who went to sea for a healthy life.

BURKITT: Shut up Coleman. Have some respect for once in your life.

COLEMAN (*pauses, looks*): But unfortunately he caught a cold. And he sneezed and he sneezed . . .

BURKITT: I said, pack it in.

COLEMAN: Touchy! (*Drums fingers.*)

CHURCHILL: Wouldn't have happened if we hadn't tried to go round the Horn. (*Pause.*) Valentine was a good lad. One of the best.

BURKITT: Yeah.

CHURCHILL: Crazy this time of year.

COLEMAN: What's that got to do with anything, Churchill?

CHURCHILL: Shut up you.

COLEMAN: Not allowed to speak now, eh?

BURKITT: Knock it off, Coleman.

COLEMAN: Yes sir Mr Burkitt.

CHURCHILL: He didn't ought to have tried to take her round. Four weeks and where have we got! Precisely nowhere and one man dead.

COLEMAN: Dunno why you two pansies are crying. At least it wasn't you! Cheers James! (*He drinks.*)

CHURCHILL: You couldn't give a damn, could you. You shit.

COLEMAN: No, frankly. Why should I? Finish your grog.

CHURCHILL: I'll finish you . . .

BURKITT: Don't listen to him Churchill.

CHURCHILL: Valentine's dead for one reason and one reason only. Bligh wants to get to Tahiti by the shortest route. Never mind men get swept overboard . . .

COLEMAN: No one got swept overboard!

CHURCHILL: . . . Never mind what happens to us, never mind what happens to the crew, never mind what happens to Valentine — he'll do what he wants to do.

BURKITT: All right.

COLEMAN (*copying* CHURCHILL): Never mind.

CHURCHILL (*to* COLEMAN): Shut up you. (*To* BURKITT.) Listen . . .

BURKITT: You're wasting your time.

CHURCHILL: It's the principle of the thing. It could have been any one of us.

COLEMAN *slow hand-claps* CHURCHILL.

I'll tear you apart, you open your mouth again.

COLEMAN (*tuts*): What a lot of heat over little Jimmy Valentine! Were you sweet on him Churchill?

CHURCHILL: Get up you!

BURKITT (*breaking*): Shut up both of you!

COLEMAN: Come on then Churchill. You wanna fight. Come on then.

BURKITT (*getting in between the two men*): For Christ's sake, knock it off Churchill.

COLEMAN: Yeah, knock it off Churchill. Daddy says.

CHURCHILL (*throws a punch towards* COLEMAN): Out of the way, Burkitt!

COLEMAN: Come on, you can do better than that!

BURKITT (*still grappling with* CHURCHILL): Shut-up, Coleman! (COLEMAN *is smiling. Depiction.*)

NARRATION: Violent conditions make men violent and make true feelings false.
Until they can see what makes them as they are,
People channel their resentments and hatred at the wrong targets.

Break.

Depiction breaks. Costume and prop change. Actors to new depiction: YOUNG *is seated, Rousseau's Social Contract to his side, brooding.* CHRISTIAN *stands at a distance looking towards him.*

Question three. How was it that some officers — so different in class from the crew — also took part in the mutiny? Tahiti. Half-way round the world. Fletcher Christian — later, leader of the mutiny. Aged 21. And Ned Young, also 21. Midshipmen — trainee officers. On board the *Bounty*.

CHRISTIAN: What's wrong Ned?

YOUNG: Nothing.

CHRISTIAN: Come on. Something's the matter. I saw you come down.

YOUNG: Nothing. (*Picking up book.*) Just wanted to read my book, that's all.

There is a pause.

CHRISTIAN: The men are bringing the breadfruit plants on board. Should be leaving soon.

YOUNG (*takes no notice. Still looking at book*): 'Man is born free, and everywhere he is in chains.'

CHRISTIAN: Come on Ned. What's on your mind?

YOUNG: Don't you see anything?!

CHRISTIAN: I don't know what you mean.

YOUNG: No.

CHRISTIAN: Look . . .

YOUNG (*interrupting*): It's just a job to us isn't it! A career. One foot on the ladder. Doesn't it worry you, what we're doing?

CHRISTIAN: No. Why should it?

YOUNG: We give these wonderful, contented people a sack of nails and a handful of glass beads in exchange for God knows how many breadfruit plants. A shipful.

CHRISTIAN: They're pleased.

YOUNG: For what? Do *they* know what they're for? To feed slaves? Do they know that?

CHRISTIAN: I don't know. Why does it upset you so?!

YOUNG: Have you ever seen slaves Fletcher?

CHRISTIAN: No.

YOUNG: Well I have. On my father's estate. I've seen them chained up like dogs at night. Women in one hut, men in another. Kept apart. I've seen my father's manager select the best stock, to put them together to breed — like cattle. I've seen that. And I've seen them whipped in the fields till they drop, because they stopped to straighten their backs. I've seen a man skinned alive by an overseer — in front of women — just for having looked him in the eyes. I've seen men and women too ill to work or too old, taken out and shot and their carcasses chopped up by others — to feed to the pigs. People, just like them up there who so generously give us their hospitality and so innocently exchange these breadfruits for a handful of beads.

Pause.

CHRISTIAN: There's nothing we can do about it Ned.

YOUNG: No. (*In despair.*) That's what so awful. We're all in it. Caught up in the whole (*searching for the word*) . . . system. We're in chains too. All of us.

CHRISTIAN: Didn't you know what the *Bounty*'s trip was for?

YOUNG: No. Then I tried not to think about it. Now I can't stop thinking about it.

CHRISTIAN (*after pause*): Well at least the breadfruits will be better food than what they get at the moment.

YOUNG: *Cheaper* food!

CHRISTIAN: Yes. But better too.

YOUNG: So they can drive them harder. Get more work out of them.

CHRISTIAN: You're not going to tell the natives, are you Ned? Bligh's strictly . . .

YOUNG: No. What's the point. (*He picks up his book and begins to read.*)

CHRISTIAN: What's the book?

YOUNG: Rousseau. *The Social Contract.* Got it in Portsmouth just before we left.

CHRISTIAN: Better not let Bligh see you reading it! *The Times* said it was a scandalous book.

YOUNG: Bligh can go and . . . (*He turns, smiles at* CHRISTIAN, *turns back to the book.*)

CHRISTIAN: Can I read it? (YOUNG *looks at him.*) When you've finished it.

Depiction.

NARRATION: A brutal system not only bears down upon the millions of working people.
But also upon those who yet have leisure to *think* about the world.
While ideas change nothing by themselves,
The right ideas at the right time are as dangerous as a bullet in a gun.

Break.

Depiction breaks. Costume and prop change.
New depiction: BLIGH *stands by the mast, imperious, strong.* FRYER *is below*
him on the ground having just appeared on deck. He is very angry but concealing it
because of the situation. LEBOGUE *is standing facing* BLIGH. BURKITT *will take*
up a similar position. Both impassive.

Question four. How much room did they have to lodge their grievances with the
Captain or protest about anything they didn't like? Fryer — ship's master. Bligh's
second-in-command. (BURKITT *walks into depiction.*) At sea again.

BLIGH. Ah, good of you to join us Mr Fryer. The men have all been waiting for you.
   Haven't they, Burkitt?

BURKITT: Sir.

BLIGH: See Mr Fryer. They've come specially to hear what you have to say.

FRYER (*confidentially*): Sir, I really think . . .

BLIGH: Do you now. You hear that men, Mr Fryer really thinks! Speak up man. Let's
   all hear.

FRYER (*after a pause*): I would prefer we discussed this . . .

BLIGH: Face the crew Mr Fryer. Face the crew. (*He does.*) Now, what were you
   saying? (FRYER *turns.*) Face the crew. Tell the men what you wrote in your little
   note. They're all ears.

FRYER: Sir, I would like to request permission to go below.

BLIGH: Request denied, Mr Fryer. We're still waiting.

FRYER (*after another pause, turning*): Sir this is really getting rather tedious.

BLIGH: Oh is it really. Lebogue — do you find this 'tedious'?

LEBOGUE: No sir.

BLIGH: There we are. It seems you are mistaken. Lebogue has told us — and he should
   know — that this is not 'tedious'.

FRYER (*on the verge of tears*): Sir, this is not fair.

BLIGH (*to crew*): Since Mr Fryer seems a little reluctant to share his thoughts as he
   calls them, with us all, it seems it falls to me to enlighten you on his behalf.
   Mr Fryer says — in his little note — that he will not sign the ship's record unless I
   write him a certificate recommending him for his service to the *Bounty*, for the
   whole voyage.

FRYER: Sir . . .

BLIGH (*a great burst*): Hold your tongue you arrogant poodle. You've had your
   chance to talk to the men. And you passed it up. (*Completely calm again.*)
   Notwithstanding Mr Fryer failed to ensure that the spare sails were in good order;
   notwithstanding Mr Fryer succeeded in guiding us into a coral reef which would
   have sunk us if we weren't copper-plated — Mr Fryer would have me write him a
   certificate of recommendation before he carries out his orders.

FRYER: That was not my fault, sir.

BLIGH: Oh really; then whose was it? Do tell us.

FRYER: It wasn't my fault. The men will bear me out. (*Looking to* BURKITT *and* LEBOGUE.)

BLIGH (*after a pause, pretending to listen*): Not very loudly. I hate your kind, Fryer. Don't give a damn about anyone but yourself. You shouldn't be on a ship – you should be in one of those Admiralty Offices, sat behind a desk, pushing a pen, filing your nails. Self-seeking parasites, all of you. Britain can go hang as far as you're concerned – as long as you're comfortable. It's your sort that lost us the American colonies. Well no more Mr Fryer! No more. I want to be proud of my country. Proud to be in the Royal Navy. And whether you find it 'fair' or 'tedious', or suiting to your delicate nature – that's what's going to happen. You understand, Mr Fryer?

FRYER: May I go now sir?

BLIGH: No. You've got a book to sign. (FRYER *goes to the book and signs it.*) Thank you Mr Fryer. Now get out of my sight, you little ponce. (FRYER *bristles.*) Oh one more thing Mr Fryer. (FRYER *stops.*) Since you find it so burdensome to carry out your responsibilities as ship's master, Mr Christian will take your place and you can have a go at cleaning the decks for a while. The men could do with some help. Dismiss the ship's company, Mr Christian.

He goes.

BURKITT: Fryer. (FRYER *looks across to* BURKITT.) Don't try and involve us again in your little games. You ain't dropping us in it.

LEBOGUE: You must be off your 'ead, crossing him.

FRYER: I don't need your advice, Lebogue. Thanks very much.

Depiction.

NARRATION: When power becomes dictatorship, even protest is an act of mutiny. Better know it then, and save your voice. And prepare to meet power with more.

Break.

Depiction breaks. Costume and prop change.
New Depiction: COLEMAN *stands with a musket aimed at* CHURCHILL. CHURCHILL *is glowering at* COLEMAN. MUSPRATT *is holding* CHURCHILL's *knees in obvious distress.*

Question five. Before they got to mutiny was any other way out tried when the pressure became too much? The crew. The *Bounty* puts in to replenish its supplies. Muspratt and Churchill take their chance of escape. Three days freedom – then they're caught. On the beach. At the water's edge. Coleman, the armourer.

COLEMAN: All right Churchill, shore-leave's over! And you Muspratt.

CHURCHILL: It's not shore-leave. Freedom.

COLEMAN: Yeah, well it's over now. Get in that boat. Captain's looking forward to seeing you again.

MUSPRATT: I'm not going back, Churchill. I can't stand it anymore.

CHURCHILL: You don't have to do this, Coleman. You could say you couldn't find us or we got away again or something.

COLEMAN: You don't think I'm going to risk my back for you, do you?!

MUSPRATT: We found a spring. Lovely clean water.

CHURCHILL: Look, what's it to you if we get away?

COLEMAN: Nothing. I'm just doing me job.

MUSPRATT: I let Sloper go, Churchill. He won't come back.

CHURCHILL: You could come with us.

COLEMAN: Yeah?

CHURCHILL: Yeah. Course you can.

COLEMAN: Really.

CHURCHILL: Yeah. There's plenty for everyone.

COLEMAN (*lowering gun*): It's tempting.

CHURCHILL: Well come on, then.

MUSPRATT: Yeah. Come on.

CHURCHILL: What do you wanna go back for, when there's all this.

COLEMAN: You jerk, Churchill. (*Gun up.*) What would I wanna go with you for, eh?! Put them manacles on and get in the boat. (CHURCHILL *is silent but murderous.*)

MUSPRATT: He was havin' us on.

CHURCHILL: Yeah I know. (*Looking at* COLEMAN.)

MUSPRATT: I ain't goin' back.

COLEMAN: I said put on them manacles.

MUSPRATT: You said we'd get away.

CHURCHILL: I'll 'ave you for this, Coleman.

COLEMAN: Put them on.

CHURCHILL: You'll have to shoot me with that thing first.

COLEMAN: You think I won't?!

MUSPRATT: I ain't goin' back.

CHURCHILL: Well go on then!

COLEMAN: Churchill. I wouldn't give you the pleasure. You put these manacles on by the time I count three or I'll shoot *him* (MUSPRATT). One.

CHURCHILL: Alright. (*He picks up the manacles and starts to put them on.*)

COLEMAN: There's a good boy, Churchill. You too, Muspratt. (*Kicks the manacles over.*)

MUSPRATT (*hysterical*): I AIN'T GOIN' BACK!!

COLEMAN: Oh yes you are!

MUSPRATT: No!

CHURCHILL: Do as he says. It'll be alright.

MUSPRATT: That's what you said before!

CHURCHILL (*handing them over*): Put them on, eh? (*To* COLEMAN.) You'd better keep your back out of my way Coleman on that ship, 'cause I'm going to get you.

COLEMAN: No you won't Churchill. You'll be down below, chained to the timbers in the galley. Then they'll hang you.

CHURCHILL: We'll see about that. (*Puts chains on* MUSPRATT.)

MUSPRATT (*weakly*): I'm not gettin' in that boat . . .

CHURCHILL (*leading him*): Yes you are.

Depiction.

NARRATION: There are no individual solutions to social problems much as we may wish it.
The system is always stronger than the individual.
And there are always men willing to serve the system,
For a few pence in their pockets.

Break.

Depiction breaks. Costume and prop change.
New depiction: NELSON *is doing a watercolour of a plant.* BROWN *is up the other end, his hands upon a plant.*

Question six. What were the tell-tale signs of the approaching mutiny? The great cabin. Stacked with the growing breadfruit plants. Hundreds of them. David Nelson — expert botanist and gardener. Brown, his assistant.

NELSON *colours.* BROWN *rubs away some aphids from the tip. He looks at the plant. Then without obvious emotion he snaps the plant off at its base. He throws the top on the floor. He looks at another. He snaps this one off too.* NELSON *hears the sound. He looks round and sees a third being demolished. Then a fourth about to be done.*

NELSON: Brown.

BROWN (*snapping the plant, then stopping*): Sir.

NELSON: What are you doing? (*Comes over.*)

BROWN: They're broken off.

NELSON (*brief pause*): Yes I can see. But why?

BROWN: Don't know.

NELSON: But . . . (*He looks at the plants and at the broken pieces.*) But why?

BROWN: Just did it. (*He walks off as though that were the end of it.*)

NELSON: Yes I know. (*Looks at* BROWN *going off.*) Brown?

BROWN: Sir.

NELSON (*looking at plants*): They're broken.

BROWN: Yes sir. (*He picks up a watering can and begins to water other plants.*)

NELSON: You must *know.* (*Pause. No response.*) I thought you liked plants . . . (*Looks at plants.*) I mean there must be a reason. Brown? (BROWN *turns to him.*)

Why? (BROWN *shrugs his shoulders.*) Are you 'unwell'?

BROWN (*slightly puzzled*): No sir. (*Goes back to work.*)

NELSON: You know I should really report this to Captain Bligh. You're not being insolent are you? (*Trying to take control.*) Brown, leave off your work for a moment and listen to me, would you? (BROWN *turns and looks, can in hand.*) I should report this to Captain Bligh. But I shan't if you promise me you won't do it again. Alright?

BROWN: Yes sir.

NELSON: You promise.

BROWN: Yes sir.

NELSON (*feels unconvinced*): Alright we'll say no more about it. (*Loses himself in worry. After a pause, patient waiting,* BROWN *recommences his watering for a moment or two. Depiction.*)

NARRATION: When things are more important than people, people are reduced to things themselves.
When a system is based on the domination of things over people,
It creates it own destruction.
For people are not things.

Break.

Depiction breaks. Costume and prop change.
New depiction: CHRISTIAN *and* YOUNG *stand, back to the mast and each other. Horror, pain on their faces.* BURKITT *is lower down, appalled.*

Question seven. If things were so bad, why didn't they mutiny sooner? Where you are sitting small canoes and other craft surround the *Bounty*. In them are men, women and children howling and moaning. Many of them are holding sharp blades and stones with which they gouge their arms and legs and faces — mutilating themselves in full view of the crew. Holding up their wounds, streaming with blood. Christian, now second in command. Young. Burkitt. (*They continue watching for a while.*)

CHRISTIAN: Why won't they stop? (*To the Nomukans.*) Why don't you stop?

BURKITT: Bligh should let their chiefs go.

YOUNG: It's pointless. (*To* CHRISTIAN.) All this for a missing grapnel.

CHRISTIAN: For God's sake, stop. She's hacking her thumb off on the side of the boat. I can't bear it, Ned. (*Looking away.*)

YOUNG: You look, Fletcher. (*Pushes his head back.*) You look.

CHRISTIAN: I can't. I'm going to be sick.

BURKITT: Bligh's off his head. He should let them go.

YOUNG: This is what you call bringing civilisation to the savages, Fletcher.

BURKITT: All this for a grapnel.

YOUNG: This is civilisation for you.

CHRISTIAN: Stop it!

YOUNG: Go to Bligh and tell him to let the men go.

CHRISTIAN: Oh God.

YOUNG: Go on.

CHRISTIAN: They won't stop.

YOUNG: Go and tell Bligh.

BURKITT: This isn't on Mr Christian.

CHRISTIAN: Oh God.

BURKITT: It's not right.

YOUNG: Fletcher.

CHRISTIAN: All right! (*At this moment* COLEMAN *arrives.*)

COLEMAN: Mr Christian, the Captain says to tell the men to take up arms. Prepare to fire on the savages.

YOUNG: What?!
BURKITT: Oh no.

YOUNG: You can't do it Fletcher.

CHRISTIAN (*paralysed*): I . . .

COLEMAN: It's an order sir.

CHRISTIAN: Very well, Coleman.

BURKITT: We don't want to do it, Mr Christian.

CHRISTIAN: Hold your tongue, Burkitt.

YOUNG: Fletcher, you can't do this. Tell Bligh you won't give the order.

CHRISTIAN: I have to.

YOUNG: Look at them. Look. Are they attacking us?!

COLEMAN: What shall I tell Captain Bligh, sir?

   CHRISTIAN *screams.*

YOUNG: Fletcher . . .

CHRISTIAN: Get out of my way, Ned.

YOUNG: Don't do it!

CHRISTIAN: You monster, Bligh!

YOUNG: You don't have to.

CHRISTIAN: Burkitt, take arms. (BURKITT *hesitates.*) Now! Or so help me I'll kill you. (COLEMAN *exits.*)

YOUNG: Traitor.

CHRISTIAN: TAKE ARMS!

BURKITT: Sir. (*He starts to go.*)

CHRISTIAN: Ned. Save me.

   Depiction.

NARRATION: Even when things pass the point of unbearability,
   Even when our moral senses are outraged by the most barbaric cruelty,
   The absence of the right leadership inevitably leads
   To submission to the rule of those who already lead.

   Break.

   Depiction breaks. Costume and prop change.
   New depiction: BLIGH *is standing by the hatch where his coconuts are stored.*
   CHRISTIAN *is standing by him.* QUINTAL *faces them.*

   Question eight. What was the final straw that turned the crew and Fletcher

Christian from private opposition to open rebellion? On board — ship's company assembled. Quintal, an able seaman. Bligh and Christian. The day before.

BLIGH: Open it, would you, Mr Christian.

CHRISTIAN: Quintal. Open it. (QUINTAL *lifts the lid.*)

BLIGH: Well then Mr Christian, what do you see?

CHRISTIAN: Your coconut store.

BLIGH: Good. Anything else you notice?

CHRISTIAN: No sir.

BLIGH: Some of them are missing.

CHRISTIAN: Missing sir?

BLIGH: Yes, missing. What do you make of that?

CHRISTIAN: Are you sure sir?

BLIGH: We have a thief abroad.

CHRISTIAN: A thief?

BLIGH: Don't keep repeating everything I say man. I tell you we have a thief. Not that that is anything unusual. This swinish mob is made up of thieves.

CHRISTIAN: I really don't think anyone would steal your coconuts sir. They have plenty of their own.

BLIGH: I tell you they have stolen them. Do you doubt me?

CHRISTIAN: No sir, it's just that it seems — unlikely.

BLIGH: Oh does it now? They were stolen on your watch, Mr Christian. Does that — 'seem unlikely'? (*Brief pause.*) What do you have to say to that?!

CHRISTIAN: I really don't know what to say.

BLIGH: So it seems. Question your men.

CHRISTIAN: Very well, sir.

BLIGH: Now.

CHRISTIAN (*brief pause*): I hardly think sir anyone could admit to theft under the present circumstances. In front of everyone else.

BLIGH: Oh. Quintal. You were on Mr Christian's watch. How many did you steal? (QUINTAL *tenses.*)

CHRISTIAN: Sir . . .

BLIGH (*over-riding*): How many did you steal?

QUINTAL: None sir.

BLIGH: Don't you speak to me like that, you ignorant piece of shit. How many?

QUINTAL: I told you sir. None.

BLIGH: Very well. Who did you *see* take my coconuts?

CHRISTIAN: He can't give names in front of . . .

BLIGH: He'll do as he's told. (*Continues to look at* QUINTAL.)

QUINTAL: No one sir. Mr Christian had one. But he never stole any.

BLIGH (*triumphant*): Oh so it all becomes clear. Mr Innocent himself! (*Looks to* CHRISTIAN.) What have you to say to that, Mr Christian?

CHRISTIAN (*in some confusion*): I was dry. I thought it of no consequence. I had one only.

BLIGH: Oh didn't you! Theft from me is of no consequence, is it not?

CHRISTIAN (*in disbelief*): It wasn't theft sir. I have plenty in my cabin.

BLIGH: Mr Christian — you are a thief, a scoundrel and a liar.

CHRISTIAN: I must object sir to this treatment.

BLIGH: Mr Christian, you will shut your trap.

CHRISTIAN: This is completely unacceptable.

BLIGH: Go below.

CHRISTIAN: Not before I have an apology.

BLIGH: That is an order. Go below.

CHRISTIAN: Why are you treating me . . .

BLIGH (*cutting in*): Or I'll have you flogged, officer or no. (CHRISTIAN *hesitates a moment then starts to go.*) Now then. That's one coconut accounted for. Who stole the rest? (CHRISTIAN *pauses.*) Go below Mr Christian. (*He goes.*) Now then, I'm waiting. (*Considerable wait.*) Very well. Mr Fryer, have the men bring up all their coconuts and other gifts and traded goods and place them in my hold. (*Pointing to the hatch.*) And Mr Christian's. We'll see how you like it. (QUINTAL *tenses* – BLIGH *sees it.*) Ship's company dismissed. (QUINTAL *stares at* BLIGH *which* BLIGH *returns with a smile, then begins to go. Depiction.*)

NARRATION: The smallest things cause revolts, if they hit at the heart of a people's being.
The interests and rights of each individual are won by social means.
Take away those rights, you produce a social force more powerful
Than he or she who takes away their rights.

Break.

Depiction breaks. Prop change.
New depiction: CHRISTIAN *is standing by the mast watching the sun come up.*
BURKITT *has just appeared on deck and is about to walk towards him.*

Question nine. Was it hard to start the mutiny? Early morning. The sun rises on an azure sea. Christian watches. Burkitt comes to him. Both think only of one thing.

Very long pause – perhaps a minute.

CHRISTIAN (*finally*): Burkitt, tell Mr Coleman to send me the keys to the arms chest.

BURKITT: Sir. (*He starts to go. Depiction.*)

NARRATION: Thinking about doing difficult things is very hard;
You might even think they're impossible.
Doing them is quite different. Suddenly it's easy.

Hold the depiction.

Break.

Depiction breaks, prop change.

New depiction: BLIGH *is being held by* BURKITT *and* CHURCHILL, *tied by his wrists, his nightshirt caught up in the tie. Resisting.* CHRISTIAN *is behind carrying a cutlass and musket.*

Question ten. What was taking over the ship like? Bligh has been seized in his cabin, dragged kicking and screaming in his nightshirt. By Burkitt and Churchill, newly released from his chains.

There is a general mêléé out of which –

CHRISTIAN: Take him up there. (*Indicating mast area.*)

More mêléé as they drag him up, all four speaking simultaneously during which finally CHRISTIAN *establishes his dominance. The sense of chaos is much more important than the audience hearing any particular lines. To achieve this effect however the scene requires concrete and very specific thinking by the actors. Lines are provided for this purpose.*

BLIGH: You'll pay for this you treacherous dogs. Let go of me. Norton. Quintal seize these men. I'll see you hang Christian! I'll make you eat bullets! Come back here you cowardly scum! You won't get away with this. I'll tear your heart out and feed it to the dogs, Churchill, you see if I don't. Mr Hayward. Seize these men. That's an order. Where the hell's Fryer!

CHRISTIAN: Alright take the musket. See he doesn't move. Shut your mouth you! Get down there. Now listen everybody. We've taken command of this ship. You'll take your orders from me. Quintal – you'll find Mr Young by the arms chest – go down and – shut up Bligh – go down and bring all the arms up here and give them to those that are with us. You open your mouth again Bligh and I'll run you through I swear to you. The rest of you – if you don't want to join us, you won't be harmed if you don't resist. Otherwise you'll suffer the consequences.

BURKITT: Hold your racket, Bligh. (*He gets down, taking the musket.*) Or you'll get a bullet through your head. I told you to shut up. Stay where you are Norton. Muspratt go and get Brown up here.

CHURCHILL: Not so big now eh Bligh? Come here. (*Wrenching him round.*) See how you like manacles cutting your wrists in half.

CHRISTIAN: Alright, Burkitt?

BURKITT: Fine, Mr Christian! Just fine. (*To* BLIGH.) Turn round and face me, you.

CHURCHILL: Eh! Look at his bum. W'hay!

BLIGH: You ignorant slob! (*Keeping his imperious posture.*)

CHURCHILL: Lovely lily-white bum, lads!

BURKITT: Stop that, Churchill.

CHURCHILL: What for?! Anyone want to take a pot-shot?!

BURKITT: I said pack it in.

CHURCHILL: Someone get Coleman up – sure he'd like to lick it!

BURKITT (*has already put his gun down and started to move towards* BLIGH): Enough.

CHRISTIAN: Burkitt. Stay where you are!

BURKITT: We're not making a spectacle of him. (*Continuing, unpicking the nightshirt.*) We're not having any of that.

CHURCHILL: Spoilsport.

BURKITT (*going back to his weapon*): You said it. Someone get him his clothes.

BLIGH: You don't impress me Burkitt. So don't think you do.

BURKITT: It's nothing to do with you. Right?

Depiction.

NARRATION: Taking power is not an act against persons.
It is not the person in power that's the problem,
But the power in the person — however it may seem.

Break.

Depiction breaks. Costume and prop change.
New depiction: LEBOGUE *is in semi-hiding, below decks.* COLEMAN *is holding a cutlass and a musket, drumming up a party for a counter-attack. He catches sight of* LEBOGUE.

Question eleven. What did those who did not mutiny do and did they pose a threat to the mutiny? Below decks. At the same time as Bligh is taken on deck. Coleman, the armourer. And under there, Lebogue.

COLEMAN: All right. Out of there.

LEBOGUE: Coleman, what's going on?

COLEMAN: Lebogue. Come on out.

LEBOGUE: Why what's happening?

COLEMAN (*grabbing hold of him* — LEBOGUE *starts to emerge*): Come on! They're having their little revolution, that's what. Now take this. (*Thrusting the musket to him.*) And pissin' hurry up.

LEBOGUE: Why can't you let him stew in his own juice? It'll sort itself out.

COLEMAN: Take it! (LEBOGUE *does.*) Now listen you. We've got some scum to hurt. And a Captain to get free. And I'm not going up there to get strung up by the testicles. Alright. Now follow me.

LEBOGUE: Is it just us?!

COLEMAN: Don't be stupid. Fryer's getting the others together. Now get going.

They go. BROWN *and* MUSPRATT *take up positions.*

NARRATION: Brown and Muspratt are posted at the hatchway onto the deck.

COLEMAN: You ready?

LEBOGUE: Yeah. I'm ready.

COLEMAN: We'll soon sort this lot out. When we hit the hatch doors, scream for all you're worth and shoot to hit Christian. Right?

LEBOGUE: Yeah.

COLEMAN: Let's go!

They both scream as they enter the deck but they are met by BROWN *who is brandishing a large piece of timber.* MUSPRATT *comes from behind and aims his pistol at* LEBOGUE. *The scream dies in* LEBOGUE's *throat, and he surrenders immediately.* COLEMAN *has not seen this as he is looking at* BROWN.

LEBOGUE: Alright. (*He puts the musket down.*)

COLEMAN (*about* BROWN): Shoot him, Lebogue. (*He parries at* BROWN *a moment before he is aware that* MUSPRATT *is waving a pistol at him.*) Get that thing away from me Muspratt. It'll go off.

MUSPRATT: Yeah. Look Churchill I've got 'im!

COLEMAN: You little runt. Give it here. You stupid pissy . . .

BROWN (*cutting in*): Keep quiet, or I'll hit you.

COLEMAN *falls silent, but glowers at* BROWN *with supreme contempt.*

MUSPRATT (*to others*): We got 'em!

Depiction.

NARRATION: Always expect counter-attack for it always comes.
Victory goes to those who at the critical moment
Show most determination to see it through.

Break.

Depiction breaks. Costume and prop change.
New depiction: BLIGH *is still tied, by the mast.* BLIGH *is without the nightshirt. Now black as thunder.* CHRISTIAN, *cutlass in hand, is holding* BLIGH's *neck turning his face towards him in a curious way. It is as if they were about to kiss.* YOUNG *is turned away having nothing to do with them.* BURKITT *will come into the depiction at some distance with the gun over his shoulder.*

Question twelve. What was the moment like, immediately after the mutiny before they put Bligh off the ship? Bligh, Christian and Ned Young. Burkitt. (*He moves into the depiction.*)

CHRISTIAN (*tense*): You gave me nothing William, but a life in hell.

BLIGH: I gave you everything. Taught you everything. Treated you like my own son.

CHRISTIAN: You did not.

BLIGH: If thine eye offend thee, pluck it out. I pluck you out. (*He spits in* CHRISTIAN's *face.* CHRISTIAN *remains looking at him a moment, then releases* BLIGH's *neck. Silence.*)

YOUNG (*also tense*): Brown, get some men and get rid of those plants. All of them. (*He watches him go. Another pause.*)

CHRISTIAN: Quintal, lower that boat into the water.

BURKITT (*quickly*): Stay where you are Quintal!

CHRISTIAN: Do as I say! I give the orders Burkitt.

BURKITT (*to* QUINTAL): Leave it.

CHRISTIAN: I give the orders.

BLIGH: That seems *very* questionable, Mr Christian.

CHRISTIAN: Shut up, William.

BLIGH: Organise a mutiny? You couldn't organise a piss-up in a brewery! (*Laughs, scornfully.*)

YOUNG: Don't start again you.

BURKITT: We should hang him, now.

CHRISTIAN: No!

BLIGH (*still laughing*): Well said, Burkitt! Let's get to it! What do you say, Mr Christian?

CHRISTIAN: He's going in the boat.

> BLIGH *continues to laugh.*

BURKITT: We should finish him now. And all the others think the same. You can't risk letting him go now. There's land not thirty miles away.

CHRISTIAN: There'll be no more violence on this ship.

BURKITT: It's not violence; it's justice.

CHRISTIAN: No it's not! Why did we take this ship? Why did we have a mutiny? To end his tyranny. Are we now to become tyrants over him? Eh?

BURKITT: Look, Mr Christian, it's not a question of being tyrants . . .

CHRISTIAN: It will be. Once you start, there's no end to it.

BURKITT: Just hang on. Let me have me say. If we let him go, what's he going to do? He's going to make for the first ship to take him back to England.

BLIGH: He's quite right, Mr Christian. We'll hang you all! You'd better listen to him.

CHRISTIAN: I'm warning you. (*Cutlass to* BLIGH.)

BURKITT: Admiralty couldn't let it go. They'd come after us. We'd never be safe.

CHRISTIAN: He might never get there!

BURKITT: But we'd never be sure. This way we will.

CHRISTIAN: So what are you going to do about the rest?! Kill them too?!

BURKITT: No. We keep them on board. They'll come round, without him. (BLIGH.)

CHRISTIAN: What if they don't?

BURKITT: They will!

CHRISTIAN: Yes but what if they don't?

BURKITT: Then, we'll have to deal with them.

CHRISTIAN: Kill them, you mean.

BURKITT: Yes, if necessary. It's them or us.

BLIGH: Well Mr Christian, here's my throat! (*Holds his throat out for* CHRISTIAN *to cut.*)

CHRISTIAN: Shut up William or I'll throw us both in the sea. (*Turning to* BURKITT.) It will turn into a slaughterhouse, Burkitt.

BURKITT: No. That's phantoms! (*He does a whirring action with his finger to his head.*) Look, don't you think they'll do the same thing to us if you let him go. This is the BRITISH NAVY. This is MUTINY.

CHRISTIAN: Then it's better we didn't start it!

BURKITT (*height of frustration*): WE DIDN'T HAVE ANY CHOICE!

CHRISTIAN (*not really hearing, he turns to* YOUNG — *who's been listening and thinking all the while*): What do you think Ned? You've not said anything.

YOUNG: I don't know, Fletcher. I don't know.

BLIGH (*bursts into laughter again*): A fine pair!

YOUNG: All I know is, you can't override the wishes of the men. If you do, you're the same as him and nothing will change.

CHRISTIAN: No. If I let them kill him, we're the same as him.

YOUNG: No. Decisions, rules, laws — must be agreed by the people. No one man can take that from them. That's tyranny.

CHRISTIAN (*passionately*): But what if the people are *wrong*!?

YOUNG: Then they're wrong! But it *is* their will. You can't have it both ways!

BLIGH: Seems the philosophers will talk all day, Burkitt.

CHRISTIAN (*moving into action*): Quintal, lower the boat.

YOUNG: Fletcher!
BURKITT: No!

BLIGH: Here we go again!

CHRISTIAN (*puts his cutlass to himself*): Lower that boat, Quintal. (*Looks* BURKITT.) Either he goes or you'll kill us both, Burkitt.

BURKITT (*looks at him a moment*): Mr Christian, you're crazy. Lower th Quintal.

YOUNG (*going*): I'm going below.

> CHRISTIAN *looks after him. Then turns back to* BURKITT *with a his face.*

BURKITT (*a resigned smile*): You're crazy.

Depiction.

NARRATION: When the oppressed rise up and seize the power,
They're always confronted with the clash between wishes and
But that's in the way of things; that's what power's about.
So who is more fit to wield it?
The oppressed or the oppressor.

Break.

Depiction breaks.

LIVES WORTH LIVING

Written by Lawrence Evans and Jane Nash

A half day programme
For Secondary Pupils

LIVES WORTH LIVING

Over the winter of 1983–4 the Belgrade Theatre in Education Company produced a
Special Schools programme called *Tribespeople*. For most of the devising team it was
a new experience meeting and working with mentally handicaped people. We found
ourselves having to confront our own fears and prejudices and began to ask
ourselves why these fears and prejudices existed. Why are mentally handicaped
people a largely invisible part of our society? The young people we worked with on
Tribespeople were vital, bright inquisitive and pull of potential. We began to wonder
what their prospects were in adult life.

These thoughts, voiced at an ideas meeting for future in-schools programmes, led to
a decision that the company should devise a programme for mid-Secondary students
about adult mental handicap. We, having both been devisers on *Tribespeople*, and
already having a passionate interest in the subject, were elected to put the programme
together.

We had eight weeks to devise the programme so decided that we could afford at
least four weeks in research. We felt that the best way of giving ourselves a broad
knowledge of mental handicap was by getting as much first-hand experience as
possible.

We began by contacting MENCAP (Royal Society for Mentally Handicapped
Children and Adults), Coventry Social Services Department with its specialist group of
social workers and several voluntary organisations involved with mentally handicapped
people. Their help was invaluable.

At the end of our research period we had amassed many hours of taped interviews
with nurses, doctors, social workers, teachers, staff of Industrial Therapy Units, Day
Care Centres, Hostels and Residential Homes. The main bulk of our interviews,
however, were with mentally handicapped people themselves and their families. Every
family we met shared with us their personal and intimate experience of mental
handicap and without their complete openness this play could not have been written.

It is to those people that we owe our gratitude in our attempt to show and raise
questions about the way we, as a society, treat mentally handicapped people and their
families.

Our research clearly showed us what the aims of the programme should be. That we
should be confronting people's own fear, prejudice and ignorance about mental
handicap. That we should show the internal and external pressures placed on the
family. That we should examine the stereotypical role of women as carers within our
society and, most importantly, that we should show that mentally handicapped people
are people first.

Our first weeks spent amassing as much information as possible paid off. We
found that when we came to write the play our ideas and impressions poured out onto
rolls of wallpaper we had stuck around the rehearsal room. At the time this was
daunting. How were we to pull all this together? With so many issues to cover and so
many stories to tell we decided to focus on a brother and sister relationship where the
brother was mentally handicapped and the sister left the carer. Generally this followed
the pattern we had experienced in our research. Also, in concentrating on a specific
relationship all the important issues would naturally emerge, being an integral part of
that relationship.

We wrote the play through improvisation around the basic storyline of a brother
and sister on holiday a month after their mother's death. We taped, transcribed and
then re-worked these improvisations, discarding what we could not use and through
this process we arrived at the finished script.

We chose an abstract set of a sand-coloured carpet to represent the beach and nine yellow cubes to represent rocks. We wanted the set to unconsciously question our audience's perception of what was real and what was unreal, and therefore question the whole concept of normality.

We decided that the programme should consist of the play plus a hot-seating session with both characters. The hot-seating, which lasted an hour was divided into four parts: the characters individually, the characters together and finally the actors out of character. (There is a full description of the hot-seating at the end of the play.)

The reactions of our audience constantly astounded us. We hoped that they would become emotionally involved with the characters but underestimated the extent of that involvement. We found that the students identified with the pains and problems experienced by the characters. In a gentle and caring manner they tried, using their own experience, to solve Mark and Julie's dilemma. And in trying to solve that dilemma they linked the characters' lives with the way other powerless groups, including themselves, are treated by society.

If our job in presenting this TIE programme was to raise questions about mental handicap then we were successful. If it was to change the world's attitude to mental handicap, then we were sadly unsuccessful. We started this project by asking the question: what are the prospects for mentally handicapped people in adult life? We found our answer: they are few. That it is a constant fight for mentally handicapped people to be recognised as people first and that their biggest handicap is other people's attitudes.

Lawrence Evans and Jane Nash, 1987

Lives Worth Living was first produced by the Belgrade TIE Company in June 1983, with the following cast:

MARK SUTTON   Lawrence Evans
JULIE SUTTON   Jane Nash

Written by Lawrence Evans and Jane Nash
Designed by Lawrence Evans, Jane Nash, Elliott Grey Turner

Lives Worth Living went on a second schools tour in May, 1984.
with Lawrence Evans and Gill Nathanson

The Characters
Julie Sutton is 23 years old. She is an unemployed nursery nurse. It is important that she is somewhat unconventional. In the original production she was fashion-conscious with blue hair and very 'loud' taste in clothes! This was for several reasons: to show her as a part of society also pre-judged and looked down upon; to smash any assumptions/value judgements the audience may have made about her from her appearance alone; to show that carers can be non-conformists and non-conformists can be carers.

Mark Sutton is 22 years old. He is mentally handicapped. In the original production he had athetoid movements of one arm (involuntary muscle spasms). He walked with a slightly spastic gait and he had involuntary tongue movements called Tongue Thrust. (He stuck his tongue out in a downward motion.) He also spoke very loudly. There were several reasons for playing the role of Mark in this way: to give the actor a 'hook'/a way into the character; to confront the audience with a stereotypical image of a mentally handicapped person.

    To maintain the authenticity of the experience for the audience we feel that it is necessary for Mark to remain in character throughout the programme until the general discussion at the end.

Family Background
John Sutton married Mary Carr when he was 22 and she was 20. Mary was three months pregnant with their daughter Julie. Eleven months after Julie's birth, Mark was born.

    John Sutton left home when Mark and Julie were 3 and 4 respectively and some years later, John and Mary were divorced. Mark and Julie started off at the same primary school. After a year and following an assessment, Mark was moved to an Educationally Sub-Normal School (Moderate). After another year and further assessment, he was moved out of the education system and into a Junior Training Centre run by the Health Authority. In 1971, the Education Act stated that mentally handicapped people were now educable and that their schooling should be placed under the control of the Education Authority rather than the Health Authority. Consequently, the Junior Training Centre which Mark was attending became a Special School where Mark stayed until he was 18 years old.

    When Mark was 14 he went into a mental subnormality hospital for 3 months while his mother recovered from nervous exhaustion.

    Mary Sutton died of cancer at the age of 42 after a long illness — one month before the action of the play.

The action of the play takes place on a beach in Southend.

Taped voices off: The sound of the pop song 'Under Attack' by ABBA *is heard playing. Noise of seagulls and waves can also be heard. After some time:*

VOICE 1 (*off*): Hey look at him over there. Here you, Oi!

VOICE 1 and 3 (*off*): Oi!

VOICE 2 (*off*): Oi you!

VOICE 1 (*off*): Hey, hey come on. Look at me. Hey you, look at me. Look at me will yer!

VOICE 3 (*off*): We're talking to you!

VOICE 2 (*off*): Come on.

VOICE 3 (*off*): Come on then.

VOICE 2 (*off*): Come on!

VOICE 1 (*off*): Oi mental!

VOICE 3 (*off*): Funny in the 'ead.

VOICE 2 (*off*): Spazzo.

Laughter. VOICE 1 *begins a song to the tune of* 'The Conga'. VOICES 2 *and* 3 *join in.*

VOICE 1 (*off*): Let's all go to Tescos
Where Spazzies get their best clothes.
A spazzy mong, a spazzy mong.
Let's all go to Tescos
Where spazzies get their best clothes
A spazzy mong, spazzy mong . . .

VOICE 3 (*laughing*): Oi look at his face!

VOICE 4 (*laughing*): Yeah. Who let you out eh?

Laughter from VOICES 1, 2 *and* 3. *The voices fade away leaving the sound of* 'Under Attack' *by* ABBA *still playing.*

JULIE (*off angrily*): Mark, come here. Come here!

Enter JULIE *wearing sunglasses and carrying a deck-chair, picnic bag, beach sandals, a plastic 'Superman' handbag and a carrier bag.*

MARK *follows behind wearing sunglasses and carring a beach umbrella, a ball, bucket, a stereo cassette recorder with the song 'Under Attack' by* ABBA *playing in the other.*

JULIE *stares at* MARK. MARK *looks away.* JULIE *is annoyed and throws her belongings down on the beach.* MARK *copies her action.*

JULIE *begins to set up her deck-chair whilst* MARK *arranges his own things by the side of the rocks.*

JULIE *has great difficulty with the deck-chair until, totally frustrated, she throws it to the ground and moves away.*

MARK *has noticed this, goes to the deck-chair and, with no difficulty, sets up the chair.*

MARK: There y'are Julie.

MARK *goes over to his Tesco carrier bag and removes a book and offers it to* JULIE.

JULIE: Why do you let them get away with it?

MARK *looks away.*

Oh give us me book!

JULIE *snatches book off* MARK. *Sits in deck-chair and reads her book.*

MARK *then begins a series of actions to try and pacify her; all of which fail.*

He switches off the cassette recorder. He collects the picnic bag and carrier bag and waits. He picks up her Superman bag and does the same.

He notices JULIE's *beach sandals and places them by her feet.* JULIE *does not react.*

Giving up, he moves to his own things. JULIE *watches him.*

JULIE (*amazed*): What are you wearing?

MARK: What?

Pause. MARK *laughs by doing a tongue thrust.*

Clothes. Boom! Boom! Beat yer.

JULIE: Showing me up. Take yer jacket off.

LEBOGUE: Alright. (*He puts the musket down.*)

COLEMAN (*about* BROWN): Shoot him, Lebogue. (*He parries at* BROWN *a moment before he is aware that* MUSPRATT *is waving a pistol at him.*) Get that thing away from me Muspratt. It'll go off.

MUSPRATT: Yeah. Look Churchill I've got 'im!

COLEMAN: You little runt. Give it here. You stupid pissy . . .

BROWN (*cutting in*): Keep quiet, or I'll hit you.

COLEMAN *falls silent, but glowers at* BROWN *with supreme contempt.*

MUSPRATT (*to others*): We got 'em!

Depiction.

NARRATION: Always expect counter-attack for it always comes.
Victory goes to those who at the critical moment
Show most determination to see it through.

Break.

Depiction breaks. Costume and prop change.
New depiction: BLIGH *is still tied, by the mast.* BLIGH *is without the nightshirt. Now black as thunder.* CHRISTIAN, *cutlass in hand, is holding* BLIGH'*s neck turning his face towards him in a curious way. It is as if they were about to kiss.* YOUNG *is turned away having nothing to do with them.* BURKITT *will come into the depiction at some distance with the gun over his shoulder.*

Question twelve. What was the moment like, immediately after the mutiny before they put Bligh off the ship? Bligh, Christian and Ned Young. Burkitt. (*He moves into the depiction.*)

CHRISTIAN (*tense*): You gave me nothing William, but a life in hell.

BLIGH: I gave you everything. Taught you everything. Treated you like my own son.

CHRISTIAN: You did not.

BLIGH: If thine eye offend thee, pluck it out. I pluck you out. (*He spits in* CHRISTIAN'*s face.* CHRISTIAN *remains looking at him a moment, then releases* BLIGH'*s neck. Silence.*)

YOUNG (*also tense*): Brown, get some men and get rid of those plants. All of them. (*He watches him go. Another pause.*)

CHRISTIAN: Quintal, lower that boat into the water.

BURKITT (*quickly*): Stay where you are Quintal!

CHRISTIAN: Do as I say! I give the orders Burkitt.

BURKITT (*to* QUINTAL): Leave it.

CHRISTIAN: I give the orders.

BLIGH: That seems *very* questionable, Mr Christian.

CHRISTIAN: Shut up, William.

BLIGH: Organise a mutiny? You couldn't organise a piss-up in a brewery! (*Laughs, scornfully.*)

YOUNG: Don't start again you.

BURKITT: We should hang him, now.

CHRISTIAN: No!

BLIGH (*still laughing*): Well said, Burkitt! Let's get to it! What do you say, Mr Christian?

CHRISTIAN: He's going in the boat.

BLIGH *continues to laugh.*

BURKITT: We should finish him now. And all the others think the same. You can't risk letting him go now. There's land not thirty miles away.

CHRISTIAN: There'll be no more violence on this ship.

BURKITT: It's not violence; it's justice.

CHRISTIAN: No it's not! Why did we take this ship? Why did we have a mutiny? To end his tyranny. Are we now to become tyrants over him? Eh?

BURKITT: Look, Mr Christian, it's not a question of being tyrants . . .

CHRISTIAN: It will be. Once you start, there's no end to it.

BURKITT: Just hang on. Let me have me say. If we let him go, what's he going to do? He's going to make for the first ship to take him back to England.

BLIGH: He's quite right, Mr Christian. We'll hang you all! You'd better listen to him.

CHRISTIAN: I'm warning you. (*Cutlass to* BLIGH.)

BURKITT: Admiralty couldn't let it go. They'd come after us. We'd never be safe.

CHRISTIAN: He might never get there!

BURKITT: But we'd never be sure. This way we will.

CHRISTIAN: So what are you going to do about the rest?! Kill them too?!

BURKITT: No. We keep them on board. They'll come round, without him. (BLIGH.)

CHRISTIAN: What if they don't?

BURKITT: They will!

CHRISTIAN: Yes but what if they don't?

BURKITT: Then, we'll have to deal with them.

CHRISTIAN: Kill them, you mean.

BURKITT: Yes, if necessary. It's them or us.

BLIGH: Well Mr Christian, here's my throat! (*Holds his throat out for* CHRISTIAN *to cut.*)

CHRISTIAN: Shut up William or I'll throw us both in the sea. (*Turning to* BURKITT.) It will turn into a slaughterhouse, Burkitt.

BURKITT: No. That's phantoms! (*He does a whirring action with his finger to his head.*) Look, don't you think they'll do the same thing to us if you let him go. This is the BRITISH NAVY. This is MUTINY.

CHRISTIAN: Then it's better we didn't start it!

BURKITT (*height of frustration*): WE DIDN'T HAVE ANY CHOICE!

CHRISTIAN (*not really hearing, he turns to* YOUNG – *who's been listening and thinking all the while*): What do you think Ned? You've not said anything.

YOUNG: I don't know, Fletcher. I don't know.

BLIGH (*bursts into laughter again*): A fine pair!

YOUNG: All I know is, you can't override the wishes of the men. If you do, you're the same as him and nothing will change.

CHRISTIAN: No. If I let them kill him, we're the same as him.

YOUNG: No. Decisions, rules, laws — must be agreed by the people. No one man can take that from them. That's tyranny.

CHRISTIAN (*passionately*): But what if the people are *wrong*!?

YOUNG: Then they're wrong! But it *is* their will. You can't have it both ways!

BLIGH: Seems the philosophers will talk all day, Burkitt.

CHRISTIAN (*moving into action*): Quintal, lower the boat.

YOUNG: Fletcher!
BURKITT: No!

BLIGH: Here we go again!

CHRISTIAN (*puts his cutlass to himself*): Lower that boat, Quintal. (*Looks to* BURKITT.) Either he goes or you'll kill us both, Burkitt.

BURKITT (*looks at him a moment*): Mr Christian, you're crazy. Lower the boat, Quintal.

YOUNG (*going*): I'm going below.

CHRISTIAN *looks after him. Then turns back to* BURKITT *with a question in his face.*

BURKITT (*a resigned smile*): You're crazy.

Depiction.

NARRATION: When the oppressed rise up and seize the power,
They're always confronted with the clash between wishes and necessity.
But that's in the way of things; that's what power's about.
So who is more fit to wield it?
The oppressed or the oppressor.

Break.

Depiction breaks.

LIVES WORTH LIVING

Written by Lawrence Evans and Jane Nash

A half day programme
For Secondary Pupils

LIVES WORTH LIVING

Over the winter of 1983–4 the Belgrade Theatre in Education Company produced a Special Schools programme called *Tribespeople.* For most of the devising team it was a new experience meeting and working with mentally handicapped people. We found ourselves having to confront our own fears and prejudices and began to ask ourselves why these fears and prejudices existed. Why are mentally handicapped people a largely invisible part of our society? The young people we worked with on *Tribespeople* were vital, bright inquisitive and pull of potential. We began to wonder what their prospects were in adult life.

These thoughts, voiced at an ideas meeting for future in-schools programmes, led to a decision that the company should devise a programme for mid-Secondary students about adult mental handicap. We, having both been devisers on *Tribespeople,* and already having a passionate interest in the subject, were elected to put the programme together.

We had eight weeks to devise the programme so decided that we could afford at least four weeks in research. We felt that the best way of giving ourselves a broad knowledge of mental handicap was by getting as much first-hand experience as possible.

We began by contacting MENCAP (Royal Society for Mentally Handicapped Children and Adults), Coventry Social Services Department with its specialist group of social workers and several voluntary organisations involved with mentally handicapped people. Their help was invaluable.

At the end of our research period we had amassed many hours of taped interviews with nurses, doctors, social workers, teachers, staff of Industrial Therapy Units, Day Care Centres, Hostels and Residential Homes. The main bulk of our interviews, however, were with mentally handicapped people themselves and their families. Every family we met shared with us their personal and intimate experience of mental handicap and without their complete openness this play could not have been written.

It is to those people that we owe our gratitude in our attempt to show and raise questions about the way we, as a society, treat mentally handicapped people and their families.

Our research clearly showed us what the aims of the programme should be. That we should be confronting people's own fear, prejudice and ignorance about mental handicap. That we should show the internal and external pressures placed on the family. That we should examine the stereotypical role of women as carers within our society and, most importantly, that we should show that mentally handicapped people are people first.

Our first weeks spent amassing as much information as possible paid off. We found that when we came to write the play our ideas and impressions poured out onto rolls of wallpaper we had stuck around the rehearsal room. At the time this was daunting. How were we to pull all this together? With so many issues to cover and so many stories to tell we decided to focus on a brother and sister relationship where the brother was mentally handicapped and the sister left the carer. Generally this followed the pattern we had experienced in our research. Also, in concentrating on a specific relationship all the important issues would naturally emerge, being an integral part of that relationship.

We wrote the play through improvisation around the basic storyline of a brother and sister on holiday a month after their mother's death. We taped, transcribed and then re-worked these improvisations, discarding what we could not use and through this process we arrived at the finished script.

We chose an abstract set of a sand-coloured carpet to represent the beach and nine yellow cubes to represent rocks. We wanted the set to unconsciously question our audience's perception of what was real and what was unreal, and therefore question the whole concept of normality.

We decided that the programme should consist of the play plus a hot-seating session with both characters. The hot-seating, which lasted an hour was divided into four parts: the characters individually, the characters together and finally the actors out of character. (There is a full description of the hot-seating at the end of the play.)

The reactions of our audience constantly astounded us. We hoped that they would become emotionally involved with the characters but underestimated the extent of that involvement. We found that the students identified with the pains and problems experienced by the characters. In a gentle and caring manner they tried, using their own experience, to solve Mark and Julie's dilemma. And in trying to solve that dilemma they linked the characters' lives with the way other powerless groups, including themselves, are treated by society.

If our job in presenting this TIE programme was to raise questions about mental handicap then we were successful. If it was to change the world's attitude to mental handicap, then we were sadly unsuccessful. We started this project by asking the question: what are the prospects for mentally handicapped people in adult life? We found our answer: they are few. That it is a constant fight for mentally handicapped people to be recognised as people first and that their biggest handicap is other people's attitudes.

Lawrence Evans and Jane Nash, 1987

Lives Worth Living was first produced by the Belgrade TIE Company in June 1983, with the following cast:

MARK SUTTON   Lawrence Evans
JULIE SUTTON   Jane Nash

Written by Lawrence Evans and Jane Nash
Designed by Lawrence Evans, Jane Nash, Elliott Grey Turner

Lives Worth Living went on a second schools tour in May, 1984
with Lawrence Evans and Gill Nathanson

The Characters

Julie Sutton is 23 years old. She is an unemployed nursery nurse. It is important that she is somewhat unconventional. In the original production she was fashion-conscious with blue hair and very 'loud' taste in clothes! This was for several reasons: to show her as a part of society also pre-judged and looked down upon; to smash any assumptions/value judgements the audience may have made about her from her appearance alone; to show that carers can be non-conformists and non-conformists can be carers.

Mark Sutton is 22 years old. He is mentally handicapped. In the original production he had athetoid movements of one arm (involuntary muscle spasms). He walked with a slightly spastic gait and he had involuntary tongue movements called Tongue Thrust. (He stuck his tongue out in a downward motion.) He also spoke very loudly. There were several reasons for playing the role of Mark in this way: to give the actor a 'hook'/a way into the character; to confront the audience with a stereotypical image of a mentally handicapped person.

To maintain the authenticity of the experience for the audience we feel that it is necessary for Mark to remain in character throughout the programme until the general discussion at the end.

Family Background

John Sutton married Mary Carr when he was 22 and she was 20. Mary was three months pregnant with their daughter Julie. Eleven months after Julie's birth, Mark was born.

John Sutton left home when Mark and Julie were 3 and 4 respectively and some years later, John and Mary were divorced. Mark and Julie started off at the same primary school. After a year and following an assessment, Mark was moved to an Educationally Sub-Normal School (Moderate). After another year and further assessment, he was moved out of the education system and into a Junior Training Centre run by the Health Authority. In 1971, the Education Act stated that mentally handicapped people were now educable and that their schooling should be placed under the control of the Education Authority rather than the Health Authority. Consequently, the Junior Training Centre which Mark was attending became a Special School where Mark stayed until he was 18 years old.

When Mark was 14 he went into a mental subnormality hospital for 3 months while his mother recovered from nervous exhaustion.

Mary Sutton died of cancer at the age of 42 after a long illness — one month before the action of the play.

The action of the play takes place on a beach in Southend.

Taped voices off: The sound of the pop song 'Under Attack' by ABBA is heard playing. Noise of seagulls and waves can also be heard. After some time:

VOICE 1 (*off*): Hey look at him over there. Here you, Oi!

VOICE 1 and 3 (*off*): Oi!

VOICE 2 (*off*): Oi you!

VOICE 1 (*off*): Hey, hey come on. Look at me. Hey you, look at me. Look at me will yer!

VOICE 3 (*off*): We're talking to you!

VOICE 2 (*off*): Come on.

VOICE 3 (*off*): Come on then.

VOICE 2 (*off*): Come on!

VOICE 1 (*off*): Oi mental!

VOICE 3 (*off*): Funny in the 'ead.

VOICE 2 (*off*): Spazzo.

Laughter. VOICE 1 *begins a song to the tune of* 'The Conga'. VOICES 2 and 3 *join in.*

VOICE 1 (*off*): Let's all go to Tescos
Where Spazzies get their best clothes.
A spazzy mong, a spazzy mong.
Let's all go to Tescos
Where spazzies get their best clothes
A spazzy mong, spazzy mong . . .

VOICE 3 (*laughing*): Oi look at his face!

VOICE 4 (*laughing*): Yeah. Who let you out eh?

Laughter from VOICES 1, 2 and 3. *The voices fade away leaving the sound of* 'Under Attack' *by* ABBA *still playing.*

JULIE (*off angrily*): Mark, come here. Come here!

Enter JULIE *wearing sunglasses and carrying a deck-chair, picnic bag, beach sandals, a plastic 'Superman' handbag and a carrier bag.*

MARK *follows behind wearing sunglasses and carring a beach umbrella, a ball, bucket, a stereo cassette recorder with the song 'Under Attack' by* ABBA *playing in the other.*

JULIE *stares at* MARK. MARK *looks away.* JULIE *is annoyed and throws her belongings down on the beach.* MARK *copies her action.*

JULIE *begins to set up her deck-chair whilst* MARK *arranges his own things by the side of the rocks.*

JULIE *has great difficulty with the deck-chair until, totally frustrated, she throws it to the ground and moves away.*

MARK *has noticed this, goes to the deck-chair and, with no difficulty, sets up the chair.*

MARK: There y'are Julie.

MARK *goes over to his Tesco carrier bag and removes a book and offers it to* JULIE.

JULIE: Why do you let them get away with it?

MARK *looks away.*

Oh give us me book!

JULIE *snatches book off* MARK. *Sits in deck-chair and reads her book.*

MARK *then begins a series of actions to try and pacify her; all of which fail.*

He switches off the cassette recorder. He collects the picnic bag and carrier bag and waits. He picks up her Superman bag and does the same.

He notices JULIE's *beach sandals and places them by her feet.* JULIE *does not react.*

Giving up, he moves to his own things. JULIE *watches him.*

JULIE (*amazed*): What are you wearing?

MARK: What?

Pause. MARK *laughs by doing a tongue thrust.*

Clothes. Boom! Boom! Beat yer.

JULIE: Showing me up. Take yer jacket off.

MARK: What.

JULIE: It's summer. You wear summer clothes cos it's hot.

MARK: Oh. (*Takes off his jacket.*) This? (*Pointing at his slip-over.*)

JULIE: Yeah.

MARK *tries to take off his slip-over. He gets it half off but becomes stuck. He moves to* JULIE.

MARK: Pull. Ta! (*Puts jumper with his jacket.*) There!

JULIE: Tie.

MARK: What?

Notices his tie and removes it. JULIE *goes back to her book.*

Shoes and socks?

JULIE: Yeah go on, live dangerously!

MARK *sits and unties laces.*

MARK: Pull, pull, pull. There! (*He throws the first shoe behind him. He then decides to pull off his second shoe without bothering to untie the laces. He throws the second shoe behind him. He then removes his socks. Gleefully waggling his toes.*) Yeah! (MARK *then notices that* JULIE's *trousers are rolled up. He does the same to his. Finally notices the audience. Removing his sunglasses he jumps up and rushes straight to a member of the audience. Holding out his hand.*) Hello! What's your name? . . . My name's Mark. How ja do. (*He shakes hands.*) Are you on holiday? I am. We bin here a week. (*He moves to another member of the audience.*) Hello! What's your name? . . . My name's Mark. How ja do. (*He shakes hands. Pointing to a third member of the audience.*) You're nice! Yeah. (*He then notices the centre section of the audience and goes over to them.*) Hello, what's your name? . . . My name's Mark. How ja do. Do you like dancin'? . . . I do! Julie took me to a disco last week. It was fun. Didn't play no ABBA though. They're

my favourite! Stay there!! (*He goes over and gets his cassette recorder.*) D' you like it? . . . Julie and Trev bought it me. Listen. (*He plays the cassette.* ABBA's 'Under Attack' *is still playing.*) It's ABBA! (*Pause.*) Enough! (*Turns off cassette and takes it back. Returning he notices left hand audience and goes over to them.*) Hello. what's your name? . . . My name's Mark. How ja do. (*Shakes hands. Moves to someone else.*) Do you go to work? . . . I do. I work at the . . . Industrial Therapy Unit. Yeah. We do . . . light assembly. That's puttin' bits together (*he demonstrates.*) and packagin'. Don't like it. Wanna leave. Be a mechanic. Yeah! (*To another person:*) Do you go to school? . . . I bin to three schools. They're special. (*To another person and depending if male or female:*) You got a boyfriend? I got a girlfriend. She's called Denise. She works at the Centre with me. (*Pointing.*) D'yer fancy him over there? I'll fix yer up if you want. (*Throughout this,* JULIE *has ignored what* MARK *has been doing until she hears him talk about girlfriends/boyfriends. She then looks round to find something to distract him. She notices a shell.*)

JULIE: Mark, come and see what I've found.

MARK (*turning round*): What?

JULIE: Come and see!

MARK (*to audience*): See yer later!

JULIE: It's a shell!

MARK: Cor. Big innit? (*Pause.*)

JULIE: Can you hear the sea?

MARK: Yeah! (*Notices starfish.*) Look!

JULIE: Oh it's a starfish!

MARK: Why?

JULIE: Cos it looks like a star I suppose. (JULIE *brings the starfish over to* MARK.) Lovely innit?

MARK (*warily*): Yeah.

JULIE (*thrusts it towards* MARK's *face*): Touch it.

MARK (*scared*): No!

JULIE: Go on. It won't hurt you.

MARK *approaches the starfish with caution and eventually touches it. He screams.* JULIE *laughs.*

MARK: Stop!!

JULIE *stops laughing.* MARK *then attempts to pick up the starfish which he eventually does.*

JULIE: There see. Looks like a star!

MARK (*still warily*): Eey' ar!

JULIE: I'll put it back in the sand.

She goes and buries the starfish. MARK *copies* JULIE *and buries the shell. To audience.*

It's our last day here today.

MARK: I don't wanna go tomorrow, Julie.

JULIE: What d' you mean 'I don't wanna go tomorrow!' How many more times? Now just don't wind me up cos I'm on me holiday, right?

MARK: I'm not goin'.

JULIE: We've been through this Mark. You're going to Northfields!

MARK: I'm not!

JULIE: You said you wanted to go yesterday. You said it was alright.

MARK: I NOT GOIN'!

JULIE: What do you think I am?

MARK: NO!

JULIE (*getting annoyed*): It wasn't my decision, right. It was you and Mum. You decided.

MARK: NO!

JULIE: Well what if I've got used to the idea? What if I want that? What if? Now you just change your bloody mind. Every five minutes. Mum wanted that. She's not here to look after you now. . . . to wash your hair and tie your shoe laces.

MARK: Do it myself.

JULIE (*to audience*): He does this every bloody time. You never know where you are with him. He led Mum a right dance! Course the best one was when he was gonna start working at the Training Centre . . .

MARK *begins to rock backwards and forwards on his knees.*

MARK (*interrupting*): Work's borin'. I hate it.

JULIE: . . . Three weeks before the day he's due to go:

'I not goin' there, Mum.'

'You what?' she says. He says: 'I'm not goin'. I don't wanna work somewhere like that.'

She was worried sick.

Where was he gonna go?

Prospective employers weren't exactly falling at his feet!

I mean Woolworth's weren't likely to take him on filling bloody shelves!

MARK: Work's borin'. I hate it. They say you're easily pleased cos yer can't fink. Don't matter wot yer do s'long as yer busy.

Don't treat yer right. 'Fore I come away I was in the office. Stood there, four of 'em.

'What you bin doin' now Mark?'

'I 'ad an argument, sir.'

'Who wiv Mark?' 'Fred, sir.'

(*Upset and angry.*) 'He's bin arguing' with everyone. Haven't you Mark?'

'Have to stop your wages so you learn. That's fair innit?'

JULIE: So it wasn't the best place in the world! But there's no alternative.

MARK: 'Now say you're sorry for all the trouble.'

JULIE: Come the day he's due to go. He walks out happy as Larry onto the bus!

MARK (*remembering*): 'Sorry.'

JULIE (*to* MARK): Mum's bin sweatin'
for three weeks.

MARK: And in front of visitors an' all!

JULIE (*to* MARK): You're not doin' that
to me y'know.

MARK: What?

(*Pause.*)

What?

*Feels his head. He looks up at the sky.
Smells his hand and then looks up
pointing . . .*

Julie, that seagull's just shit on my
head.

JULIE (*aside*): Why don't you say it
louder so the whole beach can hear.

MARK (*shouts*): THAT SEAGULL'S
JUST SHIT ON MY HEAD!

JULIE (*shouts*): COME HERE!

MARK (*showing her his hand*): Look!

JULIE (*taking his hand*): Tut! Show us
yer head! Tut! Oh come on we'll have
to wash it out.

*JULIE takes MARK by the hand,
climbs over the rocks and goes to the
sea. She removes her shoes and jumps
in. MARK stares at the waves.*

Oooh . . . it's freezing! Come on!

MARK backs away.

JULIE: Come on.

MARK (*frightened*): NO!

JULIE: I can't do it from there can I?

MARK: NO!

JULIE: Come on.

*MARK builds himself up to jump. He
enters the sea.*

MARK (*screams*).

JULIE (*laughs*).

MARK: STOP!

JULIE (*laughing*): Do your hand.

*JULIE mimes washing MARK's head.
MARK washes his hand.*

Trust you!

Continues washing his head.

There!

MARK (*laughing; mimes scooping water
to throw at* JULIE).

JULIE: You dare!

MARK (*laughing*).

JULIE: I'm warnin' you!

MARK *splashes at* JULIE.

Oh you so and so! RIGHT!

JULIE *splashes* MARK *using her feet.*

MARK (*laughing.* JULIE *and* MARK
kick water at each other):

I give in! I give in! I'm all wet now!

JULIE: Serves you right, you started it!

MARK: What?

JULIE (*with affection*): You hungry?

MARK: Yeah!

JULIE: Come on then.

*JULIE comes out of the sea, collects
her shoes and goes back to the deck-
chair. MARK follows. JULIE unzips
the picnic bag and hands MARK a
small table cloth.*

JULIE: Here y' are!

MARK: Ta!

*Whilst unpacking the rest of the
picnic, JULIE watches MARK to see if
he can cope with laying out the table
cloth.*

*MARK spreads out the cloth,
meticulously smoothing out the
creases. He then gets up and walks
over the cloth back to JULIE.*

JULIE: Grab the plates.

*JULIE takes the paper cups, sandwich
box and packet of biscuits and lays
them on the table cloth.*

MARK *grabs the plates and follows.*

*They both sit. JULIE opens the
sandwich box and unwraps the*

sandwiches. MARK *waits expectantly.*

It's egg mayonnaise . . .

MARK *inspects the sandwich.*

. . . now don't say you don't like it cos I know you do.

MARK: All right! Wot you got?

JULIE: Same as you! There's a bottle of lemonade in the bag.

MARK: What?

MARK *goes to the picnic bag. Unzips bag and takes out lemonade bottle.*

N.B. It is important that the picnic bag has a zip to show that MARK *is capable of coping with zips.*

Any crisps?

JULIE: No.

MARK (*horrified*): No crisps?!

JULIE: No crisps.

MARK: WHY?!

JULIE (*sarcastically*): Oh I'm terribly sorry. It must have slipped my mind. Would you like me to run to the shops now and get them?

MARK: Yeah!

JULIE: Well you can whistle!

MARK (*pause.* MARK *whistles*): Boom! Boom! Beat yer!

JULIE *is not amused.* MARK *knows this. He puts down the lemonade bottle, sits and begins to eat.* JULIE *takes the lemonade bottle and tries to open it. She can't.*

JULIE: Here do that for us!

MARK (*takes bottle and opens it. It fizzes*): Fizz!

JULIE: Want some lemonade?

MARK: Yeah! (JULIE *pours lemonade.*) Enough!

MARK *drinks it down in one.* JULIE *pours some for herself.* MARK *burps. Pause.*

Pardon!

Long pause.

Why in't Trevor here?

JULIE: Didn't want him to come. He's workin' anyway.

MARK: D' you love Trevor?

JULIE: Course I do!

MARK: You always say you don't cos 'e thinks more of his car than 'e does of you.

JULIE: You shouldn't listen to private conversations.

MARK: Why not? You're shoutin'. I can't stop me ears up!

They both laugh.

I think 'e does fink more of 'is car.

MARK *laughs.* JULIE *is not amused and turns away. Pause.*

Didn't mean it. Didn't Julie!

JULIE: S' all right.

MARK: Honest. Didn't.

JULIE: I know. (*Pause. To audience.*) He doesn't miss a trick. Mind you he's right. Trevor is car-mad! Well it's his job; he's a mechanic. Makes good money. I'm trained as a Nursery Nurse — passed all me exams with flying colours. Proudest day of Mum's life . . .

MARK *notices* JULIE *is talking to the audience. He does the same.*

MARK (*interrupting*): I got a job!

JULIE: I'm talking!

MARK *grabs his shoes and moves to deck-chair, annoyed.* JULIE *continues talking to audience.*

Proudest day of Mum's life when I come home with me certificate. If she could see me now. I've bin unemployed for eight months. I worked for four years in a local nursery. Same old story though innit . . . Government cuts! Lost me job.

MARK *pulls on first shoe.*

MARK (*under his breath*): I got a job.

JULIE: Don't tell me. Tell them.

(*Indicates audience.*)

MARK: What? (*Pause.*) I got a job! I'm somebody. It's like Mister Johnson says: 'you're worth somethin', you get a wage.'

JULIE: And what if you didn't have a job. Wouldn't you be worth anything?

MARK: What? (*Pause.*) Don't know.

JULIE: I haven't got a job. I'm still worth something aren't I?

MARK: What? Yeah!

JULIE: It's a lie then innit? Being somebody isn't dependent on havin' a job y'know.

Pause.

MARK: What.

JULIE (*to audience*): Course Trevor thinks he's got it sussed:

'Have a baby', he says.

Easy as pie innit?

'Give you somethin' to do during the day.'

Oh yeah? That'd knock me off the job market for years. Mind you. I would like kids one day but when I'm ready and on my terms.

MARK *pulls on his second shoe.*

MARK: Oi.

JULIE: You talkin' to me?

MARK: When you 'ave babies, what will that make me?

JULIE: You'll be their uncle.

MARK: Uncle!

JULIE: Uncle Mark!

MARK: Will I? UNCLE MARK!! When you 'avin' one?

JULIE: When I'm ready. Now finish yer sandwich.

MARK: Don't want no more.

JULIE: There's a packet of biscuits here.

MARK: What?

MARK *goes over to get biscuits. He shakes the packet so biscuits fall out everywhere on to the cloth. He takes one.*

No crisps!

He goes to rocks.

JULIE: No crisps!

MARK: Cos you forgot.

JULIE: Cos I forgot!

MARK (*half under his breath*): If I forgot all bloody hell would have let fuckin' loose.

JULIE: What did you say?

MARK: Nuffin.

Denise had a baby. They took it away. She told me. (*To audience.*) Denise my girlfriend. She works at the Centre, packin' nails into plastic bags wiv me. She's thirty-eight.

JULIE *lies down.*

JULIE: (*teasing*): D' you love Denise?

MARK: What?

JULIE: D' you love her?

Pause.

MARK: Shut up!

JULIE: Well do you?

MARK: STOP!

Pause. Begins to laugh.

My friend.

JULIE *lies down again.* MARK *eats his biscuit. He looks around. Finally.*

Wish Mum was 'ere. She'd a liked this place.

JULIE: Yeah!

MARK (*excited*): She'd paddle.

JULIE: I miss her y'know.

Pause.

MARK (*becoming upset*): Miss her.

JULIE (*trying to distract him*): That time you brought that frog home.

MARK (*quietly upset*): What?

MARK *remembers then gets excited.*

She trod on it . . .

Both laughing.

. . . swimming.

JULIE: On a Thursday.

MARK: Yeah!

JULIE: With a packet of chips afterwards.

MARK: Yeah . . . cocoa.

JULIE: Made with milk on Fridays.

MARK: Not water.

JULIE: Yeah.

MARK: Mum singing us to sleep.

JULIE: Oh er . . . 'Edelweiss'.

MARK: Yeah . . . The pictures.

JULIE: Popcorn.

MARK: Ice cream.

JULIE: The Lone Ranger.

MARK (*shouting at the top of his voice*): TONTO! . . . (*Laughs.*) . . . Her laughin' . . . punchin' that man.

JULIE: Shouldn't laugh about that!

MARK: The Social Worker.

JULIE: Mum shoutin' at him down the street, sayin' she knew more than he did!

MARK (*laughing*): Dropped his bag. All fell out!

JULIE (*laughing*): That time you were in the hospital and you made Mum that 'orrible wicker basket.

MARK: Don't remember. No. (*With panic.*) NO! (*Calmer. Remembering.*) Dad.

JULIE: Can't remember him very much.

MARK: Shoutin', starin' at me.

JULIE: I was scared of 'im.

MARK: Hit Mum wiv 'is fist . . . made her cry.

JULIE: Better off without him eh?

MARK: Yeah. GONE!

JULIE: Out the door.

MARK: Good. (*Pause.*) Didn't like me anyway. (*Pause.*)

JULIE: Mum didn't leave you like Dad did. It's different.

MARK: Different.

JULIE: Mum had to go cos she got ill an' it's better that she died.

MARK (*into distance*): Better.

JULIE: Not that she didn't like you or me.

MARK: Yeah . . . (*Getting upset.*) . . . My friend.

JULIE: My friend . . . (*To audience.*) There were some things I never told Mum. Like why I was always fightin' at school. They used to say:

'You must be funny too cos you've got a funny brother.'

Well that didn't bother me. I knew I was all right. But let them start on Mark, calling him 'SPAZZY, MENTAL, FUNNY IN THE HEAD'. I'd get so wound up, I'd go for 'em – punchin', kickin'. I still get angry when people look at him and laugh or when mums pull their kids away from him as he walks past on the street. I mean, what do they think he's gonna do? Look at 'im! He couldn't harm a fly. (*Pause.*)

MARK (*crying*): Miss her.

JULIE (*puts her hand to her head*): What? Err . . . that seagull's just shit on my head!

MARK: What? Which one? (*Pointing.*) That one?

JULIE: How the hell do I know?

MARK: Come here.

He moves to her.

Yurr . . . it's all green! Come on.

Takes her by the hand.

We'll have to wash it out.

MARK *takes* JULIE *to the sea. He jumps in.*

JULIE: Take you shoes off!

MARK: What?

MARK *realises he's got his shoes on and jumps out of the water.*

JULIE: Oh Mark!

MARK: I'm all wet now!

MARK *removes his shoes and takes hold of* JULIE's *hand.*

Come on!

They both jump into the water. It is freezing. MARK *washes* JULIE's *hair.*

MARK: Trust you!

JULIE *looks at him. He continues washing her hair.*

There!

JULIE: Is it all gone?

MARK: Yeah.

JULIE: Are you sure?

MARK (*angry*): YEAH!

JULIE *steps out of the sea and crosses to the rocks. She suddenly stops and is obviously shocked.*

MARK *jumps out of the water and grabs his shoes.*

. . . thinks I'm daft. Not that daft!

To audience.

'Fore we came away, we went shoppin'. Bought this shirt. I picked it. Julie didn't. The shop man said: 'What colour does he want?' Didn't ask me. 'Green', she said. I picked red. That showed her! They all do it. Mrs Jenkins, down the street . . . when Mum died, she come to me and Julie. She said: 'I'm sorry to hear about your Mum, Julie. How's he taking it?'

JULIE (*obviously upset by what she sees behind the rock*): Mark. Look!

MARK: What?

JULIE: Look.

MARK: What? What you lookin' at?

Climbs onto rocks.

JULIE: There.

MARK: It's a bird . . . (*Picks it up.*) . . . It's hurt. Take it to the vet.

JULIE: Too late.

MARK: Why?

JULIE: It's dead

MARK: Dead. (*Pause.*) . . . I'll put it in the sand eh?

JULIE: Yeah.

MARK: Yeah.

MARK *takes the bird to where the building bricks are. He rearranges blocks.* JULIE *cries soundlessly.* MARK *concerned, turns to look at her.*

What?

JULIE (*stifling tears*): It's all right, Mark. Take no notice. I'll be all right.

Goes to deck-chair

MARK: What?

Notices bird again and goes back to building the sandcastle around it.

JULIE: 'Oh no, Mrs Sutton. He's a lovely baby. Nothin' wrong with him. Look at him.'

You knew didn't you Mum — that he wasn't right. But it was something you couldn't put your finger on. You just knew he was different to me — not feedin' right, crying all the time, throwing tantrums, always wanting her attention. But you didn't like to keep botherin' the clinic because they'd think you were fussin'. Another hypochondriac mother wasting the doctor's time.

To the audience.

They never told her till he was four years old. They said he was hyperactive. Well that explained all the screaming and the running around and that he might be a bit backward but he'd probably be all right if he went to an ordinary school, that he'd catch up. He didn't.

MARK *accidentally knocks down part of the sandcastle he is building.*

MARK: Stupid!

JULIE: 'Why is he like that? What did I do? It must be my fault.'

You did nothing.

'I worked until I was seven months gone.'

You needed the money!

'They told me I should drink a pint of milk a day but I couldn't afford it — I had you to look after. Perhaps I had you too close together — there's only eleven months between you.'

It's got nothing to do with that!

'I know what it is. It's a punishment!'

Look Mum, it could happen to anyone. He's like that cos that's the way he is.

MARK (*looks up*): Wot's 'e lookin' at? What? (*Pause. Resumes building.*)

JULIE (*going over to* MARK): Dad hated him. Yeah, hated him. Cos you weren't gonna be a boxer or a famous footballer, you weren't worth havin' in 'is book. Damaged goods! And whose fault was it? . . .

Turning to Mum.

'You stupid cow. Can't even get that right — can't even give me a proper son.'

Course she'd committed the cardinal sin of 'aving' a girl first!

Moves to rocks.

While Mum was ill, we used to sit and talk — Mark was out at the Training Centre. It was like when I was a kid —

after Mark had gone to bed. That was my time with my Mum. I'd pretend I didn't 'ave a brother.

To MARK

Then you'd always come down cos you'd want a glass of water or a biscuit. As if you didn't get enough attention. I only had TWO HOURS — that was MY time with MY Mum and YOU had to spoil it!

MARK (*hears this last bit*): Wot you doin'?

JULIE (*startled*): Nothin'.

MARK: What?

JULIE: Thinking. (*Pause.* MARK *resumes building.*)

JULIE (*to Mum*): I don't know what you're so worried about. You went and saw the place. It's not like a sub-normality hospital. He'll be sharing a flat with four others. He'll have his own room and he can come and go as he pleases. He'll have responsibility for the cooking, cleaning, paying bills and he'll have a say in how the place is run. He'll learn how to look after himself — become his own person. Kids usually grow up and move away you know. He shouldn't be any different.

Walking over to Mum

And then you can begin to have a life of your own. You haven't had that. Be honest. Oh I know you'll miss him but he's got the right to his own life — he's not just an appendage of you, y'know.

Pause. Wearily.

Oh listen to me. The Claire Rayner of Southend!

MARK (*looks at bird*): Why did it die Julie?

JULIE: Because it's covered in oil and it couldn't fly away.

MARK: Like Mum.

JULIE: Like me if I'm not careful. (*Goes*

over to MARK.) What you doin'?

MARK (*upset*): What?

JULIE: It's good.

MARK (*brightly*): Yeah!

JULIE: Why did you have to die now?

MARK (*to audience*): Good innit? D'you go to work? . . . I do! We start baby bottles next week. Big order from Boots. Mr Johnson says we always get work cos we're cheaper than anyone else.

JULIE: Cos you're cheap labour.

MARK: What? (*Back to audience.*) Like yer shoes! Where'd you get 'em? . . . I bet I earn more than you do.

JULIE: Keep your voice down!

MARK: What?

Back to audience. Whispers.

How much? . . . I get £4 a week. (*Notices something in distance.*) Wot they doin'? Wot? (*Climbs onto rocks.*) They're kissin! (*Pause.*) They're gettin' undressed now.

JULIE (*continues sun-bathing*): They're probably going for a swim.

MARK (*staring into distance, slowly tilts his head*): Don't think they're swimmin' Julie.

Pause

Don't stop that, they'll scare that dog away. . . Told you!

JULIE (*sits up*): What are you lookin' at?

MARK: They're havin' it off!

JULIE: You what?!

MARK: They are. That's not swimmin'. JULIE *runs and joins* MARK *on the rocks. She tilts her head and peers in the same direction as* MARK.

JULIE: They are an' all.

MARK: Told you!

JULIE (*pretending to be angry, she pushes* MARK *off the rock*): You

shouldn't be lookin'.

MARK: Well I couldn't help it. They're doin' it in the middle of the beach.

JULIE: Shh!

MARK *jumps up and down waving at the couple.*

MARK (*shouts*): We know what you're doin'! We know . . .

JULIE (*yanks him to the ground*): Mark!

Grabs a biscuit and stuffs it in his mouth.

Eat that!

JULIE *is obviously embarrassed.* MARK *continues to look between* JULIE *and the lovers. Finally:*

MARK: I hope you an' Trev don't do that. Do ya?

JULIE: You should mind your own business, you cheeky monkey!

MARK: You ask me what I do with Denise.

JULIE: That's different.

MARK: Why? (*Pause.*)

JULIE: Well you don't, do you?

MARK: What?

JULIE: You and Denise. (*Pause.*)

MARK: Not allowed. Don't let ya.

JULIE: Who?

MARK: Mum. Denise's Mum and Dad. People. At the Centre. See you 'oldin' 'ands, they shout: 'STOP THAT FUNNY BUSINESS!'

JULIE (*thinking to herself*): I've thought of buying him sex.

MARK: It'll be fun livin' wiv you and Trevor.

JULIE: But you're not goin' to live with me and Trevor.

MARK: Yes I am.

JULIE: Where'd you get that idea?

MARK: What?

JULIE: Where'd you get that idea?

MARK: I thought it.

JULIE: You're going tomorrow, remember.

MARK: I'm not.

JULIE: Look, don't you understand. I don't want to be with you all the time. You get in the way.

MARK: YOU get in the way you do!

JULIE: You're noisy. It's never quiet with you around. I can't always do the things I want to do.

MARK: Mum wouldn't send me away.

JULIE: More fool her!

MARK: She loved me.

JULIE: Now don't start that. You overstep the mark sometimes you do.

MARK: Mark! Boom! Boom! Beat ya!

JULIE: I mean it. You're selfish you are. Everything has to revolve round you, dunnit? You just put on your puppy eyes and you get whatever you want.

'Oh feel sorry for me, I'm mentally handicapped.'

MARK (*turning from her*): NO!!

JULIE: The world's not like that. People don't wanna know. I'm gonna make you take charge of your own life if it kills me!

MARK (*trying to get away*): I'm not goin'!

JULIE (*following him, she grabs him*): Look. Look at me. I know you're scared. I know that's why you don't want to go. But you've got to stand up for yourself. I'm not always gonna be here. Think of me for a change. There are times when I want to be with Trevor on me own. If a job comes up in say . . . Christ I dunno . . . Manchester, I wanna be free to take it . . . I don't want to be thinking of you all the time.

MARK *desperately moves away*

Look, it's hard enough for me as it is. Because everyone expects me to just give up my life to look after you. Do you know that?

MARK: NO!!! (*Moves away.*)

JULIE: Oh why weren't you born normal? I wish Mum had stuck that pillow over your face when you were little.

Pause.

MARK (*turns to JULIE and screams*): I HATE YOU!!

Lunges at her and misses, grabs his shoes, puts them on and attempts to tie his laces – he can't. He becomes more and more frustrated and angry.

JULIE softens. Turns to see what he is doing. Notices his pathetic inability to tie his shoe laces and goes towards him.

JULIE: Oh come on. Come here!

MARK: No. Go away!! NO!!

JULIE (*undeterred, she leans over to tie his laces*): Mark, I just want to . . .

MARK (*gets up wildly and fights JULIE back across the stage*): NOOOO!!!

MARK is in some sort of fit. His speech is a terrified stream of consciousness. JULIE watches helplessly.

I'm not goin' in that naughty room. Can't get out. Long time. Cold. Dark. No windows, nothin'. Give ya pills. Can't fink. Sleepy. Needles in the arm.

JULIE (*advancing towards MARK*): What are you talking about?

MARK (*backing off, panic-stricken*): Don't hit me! Please! Please! Sorry! Get up now. Eat now! Toilet now! Day room now! Nothin' now! Bed now! Mess up routine!

Sorry! Sorry! Sorry!

MARK stands, jerking convulsively. Crying. Fighting off imaginary enemies.

JULIE *goes towards him trying to establish physical contact to calm him.*

JULIE: It's all right Mark. I'm here. Julie's here. I didn't know. It's all right. Ssshh! It's all right Mark. It's Julie. Ssshh!

JULIE *eventually takes hold of* MARK's *arms. His whole body is racked with sobs. Cradling him in her arms. They drop to the floor where* MARK *cries like a baby and* JULIE *rocks him gently.*

Ssshh! Come on. It's all right Mark. Ssshh! Ssshh!

She hums 'Edelweiss'. *This calms* MARK *considerably. At the end of the song* JULIE *drags him to his feet.*

JULIE: Come on. Talk to me about somethin' else. Don't cry. Come on. (*They pace.*) Come on. Talk to me.

MARK: What?

JULIE: Talk about . . . that time when you got lost and the police brought you back.

MARK: When I got lost?

JULIE: Remember: you used to get yourself lost once a week and the police would bring you back and you'd have a bag of sweets.

MARK: Oh yeah! Yeah!

JULIE: And this went on for a long time didn't it?

MARK: Yeah.

JULIE: And what did the police say to Mum in the end?

MARK: Don't remember.

JULIE: Yes you do. That . . . you shouldn't be allowed . . .

MARK: Shouldn't be allowed out on me own.

JULIE: And Mum said: 'Oh it's funny he can find his own way home four nights of the week.'

MARK: Yeah.

JULIE: And then she turned to you and said: 'Why do you keep botherin' the police?' And what did you say?

MARK: Cos they keep givin' me sweets!

JULIE: And he went all red . . .

MARK: All red.

JULIE: That Sergeant. Cos he knew you'd taken the mickey out of 'im.

MARK: Taken the mickey. Makes a change.

Pause

Stop now.

JULIE (*they stop.* JULIE *looks at him Notices his untied laces*): Oh look at the state of ya! You'll trip up. Sit down.

MARK: What?

JULIE: Sit down. (*They sit.*) (*Insistently.*) Now watch!

Takes one set of laces and demonstrates tying them. MARK *watches intently.*

Now you got your two laces right — cross 'em over — now that one has got to go in there like that, right? — now take both ends and pull — like that see — now you're going to make a loop with this one right — so watch, watch — there's your finger right — now make a loop round your finger and hold it at the bottom, right — now this one has got to go all the way round the outside — so, watch, watch — right. Now this is the hard bit — you've got to make another loop by pushing that through there with your finger — right, so you got a loop there and a loop there — now pull gently — there, see — now you have a go.

MARK: What?

JULIE: You heard!

There follows a long moment between them. JULIE *is almost daring him to have a go.* MARK *glances between* JULIE *and his unlaced shoe.*

He decides to have a go. Throughout it

*is extraordinarily difficult for him:
instruction – assimilation – carrying
out of instruction.*

Two laces – cross 'em over – cross
'em – cross 'em – right – now that
one goes in there – go on – right –
now take hold of the ends – the other
one too – right – now pull – now
you've got to make a loop like I
showed you – round your finger –
right – well hold it at the bottom –
right – now that one goes all the way
round – gently – make sure that loop
stays up – there – now you've got to
push that one through there like that –
come on, you do it! – right now you've
got the two loops, one there and one
there – now pull – pull – THERE!

MARK (*triumphantly*): YEAH!!

JULIE: I bet Denise has missed you this
week.

MARK: Spect she has. I'll buy her a
present eh?

JULIE: Yeah.

MARK: What?

JULIE: You could get her some perfume.
They do little bottles of like Devon
Violets, cologne stuff.

MARK: What? Spray?

JULIE: Yeah or just sort of dab-it-on.

MARK: How much?

JULIE: Dunno. Not much. Coupla quid
I s'pose.

MARK: 'Ow mu . . . two?

JULIE: Yeah.

MARK: I only get four.

JULIE: I'll help you out.

MARK: And a bow.

JULIE: A bow?

MARK: Yeah on it!

JULIE: Oh yeah. Yeah.

MARK: And paper.

JULIE: Yeah, wrap it up nice – she'll
like that.

MARK: Yeah. And give that. Right. You
get somethin' for Trevor.

JULIE: Huh. Oh he'll be lucky if he gets
a stick o' rock!

MARK: Buy 'im somethin' for the car!

JULIE: Bloody car!

MARK: Yeah. Buy 'im some . . . dice.
Furry!

JULIE (*laughing*): Oh no!

MARK: Yeah. They're nice!

JULIE: You like 'em do ya?

MARK: Yeah.

JULIE: I don't know about that.

MARK: Trev like 'em!

JULIE (*disapproving*): Mmmm.

MARK: He's all right Trev. He's got dirty
'ands though.

JULIE (*laughing*): What?

MARK: Oil and muck. He should scrub
'em!

JULIE: Have to use Swarfega.

MARK: What?

JULIE: Swarfega. It's this stuff that you
put on your hands to take the oil off
cos water don't take oil off.

MARK: Buy 'im some o' that.

JULIE: Not a very nice present is it?

MARK: Give 'im the hint though! (*They
both laugh.*)

JULIE: Could put a bow on it!

MARK: Yeah. And wrap it up. He'd fink
it a real present. See his face!

JULIE: You'd love to get me in trouble.
Wouldn't ya?

MARK: Yeah . . . NO!

JULIE: I don't believe you!

Pause.

MARK: Ya do!

*They laugh. MARK looks round. Spies
cassette. Says coyly:*

Can I play the cassette?

JULIE: Yeah.

MARK (*at the top of his voice*): YEAH!!

JULIE: Not too loud though!

MARK *plays around with the cassette player while* JULIE *starts to pack away picnic things.* ABBA'*s* 'Under Attack' *is on first.*

MARK: ABBA!!

MARK *fast-forwards the tape on to* 'Oh Julie' *by* Shakin' Stevens *at which he becomes very excited.*

Shakie' Stevens!!! JULIE!!!

He begins to mime along to the record doing SHAKIN' STEVENS *impressions.* JULIE *is very embarrassed. She continues to pack away the picnic things. By the end of the song she is in the deck-chair with her sunglasses on, hiding behind her paperback novel. The song ends.*

What? Bow! (*Moving to* JULIE.) Why you hidin'? What?

'Knowing Me, Knowing You' *by* ABBA *starts up on the tape.* MARK *gets very excited.*

What? It's ABBA!!! Dance, Julie!!

JULIE: Do what?

MARK: I'll teach ya to waltz.

JULIE: NO!

MARK: Come on!

JULIE (*takes off sunglasses*): All right. (*Gets up from deck-chair.*) Now I don't know how to do this. You'll have to show me. (*They face one another.*)

MARK: Right. (MARK *grabs* JULIE'*s left hand and puts it on his shoulder.*) Put that there. (*Yanks other arm and stretches it out in tango style.*) An' put that there.

JULIE (*smiling*): Right.

MARK: That foot. (*Treads on her toe.*)

JULIE: Oww!

MARK: Sorry! That foot goes that way!

JULIE: Right.

MARK: And that foot goes that way.

JULIE (*laughing because he had directed her in an outlandish direction*): Right.

MARK: Then you bring 'em together. And you count in threes.

JULIE: And . . .1 . . .2 . . .3

MARK/JULIE: 1 . . . 2 . . . 3 . . . 1 . . . 2 . . .3 . . .1 . . .2 . . . 3

They begin to waltz getting faster and more confident until:

MARK: You're leadin'!!

JULIE: Sorry!

MARK: AGAIN! And 1 . . . 2 . . . 3

MARK/JULIE: 1 . . . 2 . . . 3 . . .1 . . .2 . . .3 . . . 1 . . .2 . . . 3

They both laugh and begin to enjoy themselves. JULIE *then notices something off-stage. She breaks away from* MARK.

JULIE (*to off-stage*): What? What did you say? Come 'ere and say that! . . .

MARK (*softly*): No.

JULIE: Come 'ere and say that!

MARK *becomes agitated. He tries to placate* JULIE. *He keeps up a continuous stream of:*

MARK: Don't matta Julie. Please Julie. Don't! It don't matta!

JULIE: . . . Oh 'ark at him! Have YOU looked in the mirror lately mate? Oh naff off! YOU shouldn't be allowed on it. People like you make me SICK! Oh yeah? Up yours an' all. Up yours!

MARK: Don't matta Julie. IT DON'T MATTA!

JULIE (*rounding on MARK*): It DOES matter. DON'T let people call you names like that — I can't bear it! Just turn round and say:

'You're the ones that are mad' because they are. It's not you!

MARK (*upset*): Well?

JULIE: You've got to stand up for yerself. Those berks this mornin'. You just took it, didn't ya?

MARK: It's hard . . .

JULIE: I KNOW IT'S HARD but you've got to do it. I can't do it for ya! FIGHT BACK!

MARK *turns his back on her.*

YOU JERK! YOU SPAZZ!

MARK *puts his hands to his ears and screams.*

MARK: NO! NO! NO!

JULIE: YOU STUPID MONG! FIGHT BACK! FIGHT BACK! FIGHT BACK!

She realises what she has said and breaks down.

MARK *cries.* 'Knowing Me, Knowing You' *continues.* JULIE *regains control. She turns off cassette player.*

JULIE: D' ya fancy an ice cream?

MARK (*covering up*): Yeah!

JULIE: If I give ya the money d' ya wanna go and get 'em?

MARK: (*Nods.*)

JULIE (*goes to handbag*): Come here then. Now here's a pound. You won't want more than that. You want two cornets an' twenty pence change.

MARK: Not trumpets!

JULIE: Cornets!! And twenty pence change.

MARK: Twenty pence change.

JULIE: Off you go then.

Exit MARK. JULIE *watches him go.*

MARK *re-enters with cornets.* JULIE *picks up her paperback and pretends to read it intently.*

MARK (*offering ice cream*): 'Eeyar!

JULIE: Oh ta!

MARK: An' twenty pence change.

JULIE: Oh keep it!

MARK: Ta!

MARK *sits beside* JULIE *on the sand. They both stare at their ice creams and smile. Looking at one another, they laugh.*

They pan round the audience. Then they both plunge their ice creams to their foreheads and fall about laughing. They clean themselves up and begin to eat their ice creams.

Good!

JULIE: Ja have to go far?

MARK: No.

They eat their ice creams. It starts to rain. JULIE *notices.*

JULIE: Here y'are. Hold that. (*She puts up the umbrella.*) Give us me ice cream back! Ta!

She goes and sits under the umbrella. She watches MARK *get rained on. He slowly realises it is raining.*

MARK: Julie, it's rain . . .

JULIE (*laughing*): Come here!

MARK: What?

Notices where JULIE *is and quickly clambers towards her.*

Ya mighta told me!

Pause

This is the best 'oliday I've ever 'ad! It's FUN!!

JULIE: What time is it?

MARK: What? (*Looks at watch.*) Twenny ta five!

JULIE: Your teacher at school said you'd never learn to tell the time.

MARK: What? . . . Mum taught me. Two weeks.

JULIE: See you CAN do things when you want to!

Pause.

MARK: I don't know wot to do Julie.

JULIE: I'm not gonna make you go – it's

up to you. (*Pause. The rain stops. JULIE notices. Stands up. Goes to her bags.*) Eeyar Mark. It's stopped!

MARK: What?

JULIE (*picking up stuff*): Tell you what . . . I'll race ya!! (*Starts to run.*)

MARK: Wot?

JULIE: I'm winnin'!!

MARK: Wot?

MARK *scrambles out from under the umbrella excitedly laughing and screaming. He collects his belongings together.*

That's not fair! Wait for me! JULIE! (*Laughs.*) You 'ad a head start! Wait for me!

Taped voices off:

VOICE 1: Oh look who it is!

VOICE 2: Mong, Wally.

VOICE 3: Spazz Features.

VOICE 1: Bet your Mum had a fit when she saw you!

Laughter.

VOICE 1: Plastic Spastic.

VOICE 1 *begins a chant.*

Plastic Spastic/Plastic Spastic/Plastic Spastic.

VOICES 2 *and* 3 *join in. The chant becomes faster and faster.*

MARK *becomes increasingly agitated as the chant continues. He drops his belongings but keeps hold of his football. He keeps looking at where the voices are coming from.*

He gradually picks up courage and is about to fight back. The chant becomes louder and reaches a crescendo. MARK *finally opens his mouth but cannot speak. He crumbles and cries in anguish. He throws the ball away. It hits the sandcastle and it collapses. He runs off shouting:*

MARK: NO! NO! NO! JULIE!

The sound of 'Under Attack' *by* ABBA *is gradually heard.*

Hot-Seating Guidelines 2nd Tour: May–June 1984

Compiled by Lawrence Evans and Gill Nathanson

The following outline of how we ran our 'hot-seating' session is obviously intended merely as a guide.

We would suggest that a third person is used to organise and run the hot-seating so that the actors do not have to come out of character.

During the break, following the play, we reorganised the chairs into two semi-circles. After the audience had congregated, they were asked to divide themselves evenly between the two sets of chairs. They were also given the following information:

1. It is one week since Julie and Mark returned from their holiday.

2. Mark is supposed to be going to Northfields (a place you've heard about in the play) tomorrow:

3. You will have a chance to talk to BOTH Mark and Julie and ask them any questions that you might have.

Enter MARK *and* JULIE . . .

JULIE: Mark!

MARK: What?

JULIE: Well . . . have you made yer mind up? Are you going?

MARK: Going where?

JULIE: You *know* where!

MARK: I not decided yet.

JULIE: What d' ya mean? You were packed and ready to go yesterday.

MARK: I changed me mind.

JULIE: I don't believe it!

MARK: Well believe it! I can if I want. It's up to me!

JULIE: What about me? . . .

They part, still muttering, to go to separate groups. They spend approximately 15 minutes 'hot-seating' before swapping over groups. In our production, JULIE facilitated this.

The 'hot seating' served the dual purpose of encouraging the audience to question, on a deeper level, their and society's attitude to mental handicap through addressing themselves to the characters' concrete problem of whether MARK should go to Northfields. Both actors had specific lines to follow which we felt facilitated this process. For example:

JULIE: I can't understand why Mark doesn't want to go to Northfields.

This usually started off an argument about the need for security versus the need for independence.

JULIE: Why should *I* be responsible for Mark? Mark has a right to his own life away from me. I have a right to my own life too.

Again, this leads on to arguments about the family versus the state's responsibility to give people like MARK the help they need to achieve an independent life.

Another important aspect of JULIE's 'hot-seating' would be to challenge the notion of women in the family being the most suitable people to take the role of carers of mentally handicapped people:

JULIE: If I was Mark's brother, would people expect me to look after him? No! So what difference does it make that I'm his sister?

MARK's 'hot-seating' challenged in a slightly different way. The actor's line was to look at the concept of prejudice:

MARK: Have you got sisters? Do they talk at you all the time? What d' ya do about it?

This led to a discussion on 'Fighting Back' and raised questions such as the use of violence, both verbal and physical and ways of dealing with it.

MARK: Do people call ya names? What? WHY do they call ya names? People call ME names. WHY?

Again this leads the discussion on to name calling and why people do it and eventually on to the area of 'difference'. The difference between MARK and other people. Why people are afraid of people like MARK, and how and why that misconception is perpetuated.

Again, this leads the group to discuss the concept of power within our society. Who has power? How is it used?

MARK: Do people talk down to ya? They do it to me too! Why do people talk down to ya?

At the end of the thirty minutes, the characters and audience come together for a final few minutes in order to answer, jointly now, any final questions in character.

We then talked to the group out of character. In this last part of the session, we could try to highlight any issues raised by the audience during the 'hot-seating'. For example:

1. The position of women as carers in our society.

2. The need to label sections of our society (what the label 'mentally handicapped' means) — are labels positive/negative?

3. Because mentally handicapped people are generally 'non-producers' in our society, they seem to be treated as being worthless.

Lawrence Evans and Gill Nathanson